Men of Popular Music

Men of Popular Music

by
David Ewen

Essay Index Reprint Series

BOOKS FOR LIBRARIES PRESS
FREEPORT, NEW YORK

Library of Congress Cataloging in Publication Data

Ewen, David, 1907-
   Men of popular music.

   (Essay index reprint series)
   Reprinted from the ed. of 1944, Chicago.
   Bibliography: p.
   1. Jazz musicians--Biography. 2. Music, Popular
(Songs, etc.)--U. S.--History and criticism.
I. Title.
ML390.E84 1972   785.4'2'0922 [B]   72-6818
ISBN 0-8369-7263-5

PRINTED IN THE UNITED STATES OF AMERICA

CONTENTS

♪

INTRODUCTION

♪

INTRODUCTION

Our popular music is as old as our country. We fought our Revolution with popular songs. Our first hit was the "Liberty Song" (1768) —lyrics by John Otis, the music borrowed from William Boyce's "Hearts of Oak"—which expressed the political fever of pre-Revolutionary America so aptly that it was soon adopted as the official song of the Sons of Liberty. Our first successful composer of popular songs was William Billings (1746-1800), who earns consideration as the direct ancestor of Tin Pan Alley troubadours by virtue of his rousing Revolutionary War songs. These were adapted by Billings from his own psalm tunes and were sung extensively in camps, on battlefields, and in town halls; one of them, "Chester," is often spoken of as the "Marseillaise" of the Revolutionary War. With songs we described the birth pains of a nation, and with songs we echoed the temper of a pioneer people in the face of early social, political, and economic problems that confronted them as they led America out of her infancy.

Yet, though we can date our popular music back to the period of our national birth, it is only since the twentieth century opened that this music has acquired a personality of its own as well as musical significance. To go—as I have lately gone—through thousands of popular songs which Americans have sung since 1770

1

is to be made strongly aware of how static our popular music expression was up to 1900. The American popular song was, at its origin, derivative from foreign sources: the melody was invariably lifted directly from English, Irish, Welsh, or Scottish balladry.* And the utilization of this melody was conventionalized—in the evenly balanced phrases, in the stereotyped rise and ebb of the lyric line; rhythm and harmony were inconsequential. Even after a century, the musical progress that had been made was almost negligible. The melodies were still frequently borrowed from foreign lands, and when they were of original composition they carried within themselves the echoes and memories of a hundred other songs. The pattern was still a formal one, and the full resources of musical writing were virtually untapped.

This is not to imply that some good songs were not written in that period. One cannot overlook Stephen Foster's compositions, or the often appealing songs of composers such as Work, Root, and Bland. What Foster had—and to a lesser extent some of the others—was a high degree of melodic sensitivity and inventiveness. All of these men wrote in the formulas of their time, but because they were composers of some talent, endowed with creative powers, they were able to produce melodic shapes of rare beauty from rigid molds. But not even the best of them took any step forward.

Beginning (roughly) with 1900, however, a definite progress is to be observed in our popular music. That year marked the beginning of a notable epoch in American history. The Spanish-American War had

---

* In our time, popular song composers frequently borrow their melodies from Tchaikovsky, Grieg, Debussy, Ravel, Beethoven, Rachmaninoff, etc.; and thus the circle is completed.

been fought successfully, establishing us as a great imperialist power. Internally also there was unprecedented expansion as America achieved industrial primacy. Everywhere there were evidences of growth, development, increasing strength. It was therefore to be expected that along with such heightened self-importance America should become surer of herself, less inclined to look across the ocean for models to imitate, more determined to stand on her own feet. A national consciousness and pride swept the country —musically symbolized, perhaps, by the marches of John Philip Sousa. American writers began to write about American subjects. American composers strove toward the writing of American music and native American opera.

A similar revolution was taking place in our popular music. A new era was at hand, creating for popular music changes as far-reaching as those which were taking place in our economic, social, and political life. Melody began to adopt a richer and more individual character, first with composers such as Victor Herbert, then with Irving Berlin and Jerome Kern. Emphasis was now being placed on rhythm, which (in ragtime) developed intriguing and ingenious devices. Composers like Kern became conscious of their harmonic language, and tried to enrich it. And, after 1917, the element of orchestration began to play a major role.

Popular music, in short, began at last—and belatedly —to take advantage of the equipment which centuries of development had produced; it began to aspire toward musical significance. The illiterate composer of the Tin Pan Alley of 1890 and 1900 who played the piano with one finger and had to dictate his tunes to an amanuensis was succeeded (for the most part, though not entirely) by the conservatory-trained musician who knew what he was doing, and who knew how to do it; a careful survey will prove that today there exists a far higher percentage of good musicians among our men of popular music than there was a few decades back. As the pat formulas that had served for so many years became less acceptable, the new hit tunes aimed more and more at individual and original forms of expression.

But of greater importance was another change: our popular music acquired a national identity. Popular songs before 1900 had been, for the most part, of obviously foreign birth (I do not refer to our folk music, or to random exceptions inspired by Negro examples). Even Victor Herbert—the king of Tin Pan Alley in the early 1900's—spoke a foreign language. But the ragtime that was born in New Orleans, the blues that Handy crystallized in Memphis, the swing and the boogie-woogie evolved in Chicago—all this is so authentically American that it is impossible to conceive of them as having originated anywhere but in this country. For better or for worse this is ours, expressive of our temperament and our personality.

2.

Greater complexity of technique and increasing subtlety of expression were made possible by a reorientation of our popular music after 1900. Before then, the singing of popular songs was one of the favored diversions of the entire country. For America at large, the theater, the concert hall, and the restaurant did not play a major part in everyday social life; and the movies were not yet born. One pleasant way, therefore, of spending an evening was to join congenial friends and relatives in singing the songs of the day to the accompaniment of the parlor organ, piano, or (somewhat later) the player-piano. Song collections—called "songsters"—containing the lyrics of the most popular of the current songs had begun to be issued soon after the Revolutionary War (*The American Miscellany*, published in 1789, was the first successful "songster") and enjoyed wide distribution.

Because songs were meant exclusively for singing by the general public, they had to be simple, direct, stripped of any confusing subtlety; and, because the bulk of the public for which these songs were written were women, the songs were frequently sentimental and unctuously moral.

But after 1900 the tendency grew less and less to sing, and more and more to *listen* to, the songs of the day. The rise in popularity of wholesome theatrical entertainment—vaudeville, operetta, musical comedies, revues—was the first force to shatter the tradition of parlor singing. People continued to sing the popular melodies of the day, but the practice was no longer social or communal. And after 1910 the birth and development of mechanized music—the player-piano, phonograph, radio, and the talking screen—reduced the tradition to ashes.

Popular music was now exploited not by the masses themselves but by experienced and trained performers —singers, bands, orchestras, stars of revues and vaudeville. And it was with an eye on the performer rather than on the general public that songs were now being written. It was now possible to bring to popular music a greater variety of writing, a more adult technique. To this development might be added still another— the sudden vogue for dancing as a nationwide social institution. Popular music, in serving the purposes of the dance, inevitably acquired greater rhythmic ingenuity.

The reorientation was completed through American mechanical progress. We now heard our popular songs everywhere: in the living-room, through the phonograph and radio; in the motion-picture theater, first through the introduction of slides, then with the growth in importance of accompanied music, finally with the birth of the talkies; in the theater, in public taverns (through juke boxes), and even in restaurants (through Muzak). Never before had an entire country been so continuously subjected to so much music. Inevitably, familiarity bred contempt, shortening the life span of any poor song. A novelty might sweep the country, or a lachrymose ballad of 1890 character; but, because we were so frequently subjected to it, it could not possibly maintain, its popularity long. Whereas, whether aware of it or not, we remained faithful to songs that with repeated hearings brought new musical discoveries. It was inevitable, therefore, that the quality of our popular music should rise, and rise sharply; and that the songs whose popularity persisted from one year to the next should be those that had intrinsic musical value.

3.

Men of Popular Music traces the evolution of our

popular music during the last forty years. Because these were such decisive years for our popular music—years in which it acquired its accepted styles, integration of forms, and individuality of speech—this book at the same time traces almost to its roots the history of American popular music as we know it today.

That evolution is told through the careers, achievements, aspirations, and personalities of a dozen or so men who gave our popular music its shape and form. It is a story well worth telling. The songs America sings and listens to throw brilliant illumination upon her inmost personality. It is not only an interpretation of American musical history that we have here; it is, in fact, an interpretation of America itself. Carl Sandburg wrote with unique appropriateness that "the song history of America, when some day it gets written, will accomplish two things. It will give the feel and atmosphere, the layout and lingo, of regions, of breeds of men, of customs and slogans, in a manner and air not given in regular history, to be read and not sung."*

In order to tell this story, I have thought it both expedient and effective to select one, two, or three men who were (or are) most prominent in, and representative of, various phases of our popular music. Through their careers I describe the birth and development of each distinct phase or style. Conceivably, six historians selecting the dozen men most representative of various aspects of our popular music since 1900 might select six different lists. My own choice is not offered as definitive. It is convenient and arbitrary, serving usefully the purpose I had set for this book. I emphasize this point because some readers or critics,

* Introduction to *The American Songbag*, edited by Carl Sandburg (Harcourt, Brace & Co., 1927).

not finding here their own personal heroes, might resent what they would consider unpardonable omissions. To such, I repeat that this volume is not intended to be an all-inclusive history. It is, rather, a panorama, a *coup d'oeil* over the vista of our popular music. As such, it can gather within its focal vision only a few convenient and easily recognizable peaks. There are other peaks as well—but to have included them would have invited repetitiousness.

Men of Popular Music includes not only composers but performers as well. In this respect our popular music differs sharply from that of any other country: its development cannot be discussed without including an analysis of the achievements of some of its interpreters. Important phases of its development have been due to men who never put pen to paper—men like those fabulous ragtime music-makers of New Orleans. They developed a language, integrated a style, evolved an idiom, as unmistakably as if they had written a library of music. To have omitted men like King Oliver or Benny Goodman from our story because they were not famous as composers of songs would have left yawning gaps.

4.

Though this book was written by a music critic who has heretofore devoted himself exclusively to the field of serious music, he has not (I hope) approached his task with any attitude of condescension. It is, rather, because he has long felt that our popular music deserves the attention of even serious musicians that he undertook to write this book in the first place.

As a matter of fact, the truly integrated musician has never looked upon popular expressions in music as a lower form of art, but only as a different form. Mozart, Beethoven, and Schubert wrote popular music when they composed their *Ländler* waltzes, German and Viennese dances—for they were writing the music of the masses. Brahms and Verdi were infatuated with the waltzes of Johann Strauss. Leopold Godowsky loved Lehár's *The Merry Widow,* and he was one of Gershwin's most ardent admirers. Lotte Lehmann sings Viennese popular songs with as much seriousness of purpose and attention to style as she does the famous *Lieder.* Stokowski has been one of the earliest passionate admirers of jazz. Heifetz is a boogie-woogie fan.

It is a sign of increasing maturity that we, as a nation, are now regarding our popular music with greater respect and admiration. Toscanini conducts the *Rhapsody in Blue* and the *Grand Canyon Suite.* Iturbi plays Gershwin's jazz piano preludes at a serious piano recital. Benny Goodman's swing shares a program with Stokowski's orchestral music at the Hollywood Bowl. A special course on jazz is held at the New School for Social Research. Books analyzing jazz structure and style are written by serious musicians and presented for serious musicians. Evidently, popular music in America is no longer a stepchild, abused and ignored.

In discussing popular idioms, I realized at once that it was not possible to use the yardstick which I had for so many years adopted for serious music. You cannot, with the best intentions in the world, compare Benny Goodman or Duke Ellington with Toscanini; Richard Rodgers or Irving Berlin with Schubert, Brahms, or Hugo Wolf; Jerome Kern or Cole Porter with Wagner and Richard Strauss. Obviously, it was necessary to consider popular music as a distinct world and to adopt for it a scale of values of its own. Consequently, when I use here such words as *great* or *brilliant* or *important,* the words are not to be read as meaning what they would mean if I used them in a discussion of serious music.

After all, popular music does not aspire to accomplish what serious music does. Popular music is, primarily, entertainment; it is an avenue of escape, an ivory tower. It never hopes to uplift its listeners, to move, to exalt, to inspire, in the way that Bach, Mozart, Beethoven, and Wagner do. That this is a serious flaw—and one which must be remedied before popular music achieves greatness—does not weaken my position. In short, popular music has a sphere of its own, a limited one, but *within* that sphere it has importance and validity. You do not condemn a hill for not being an Alpine peak; each has its own scenic beauty. It would be silly to dismiss Gershwin because he was no Beethoven, or Berlin because he is not a Schubert. Within their own world, Gershwin and Berlin *are* important composers.

5.

In preparing this volume, I have been motivated by the desire to bring the full recognition of our popular music one step closer to realization. I felt impelled to write this book not only because of my personal admiration for many different styles of American popular music, but also because I have not so far encountered in print any panorama of American popular music which provides a complete and undistorted picture for the intelligent and inquisitive layman. There are many books on jazz—hot or otherwise—and some of them are brilliant. Too often, however, their authors have been biased toward one particular phase of jazz, and contemptuous of all others. The admirer of Gershwin and Whiteman forgets completely that these men owed a great debt to New Orleans ragtime; while the devotee of "hot" jazz writes as though Gershwin, Berlin, and Kern have played no part whatsoever in our popular music. I believed that there was need for an impartial historian to survey the field and to appraise what he saw. I hope that this book is such an impartial history, in which every major trend in popular music of the past forty years is given its due without prejudice.

In conclusion, I would like to express my indebtedness to those whose assistance and collaboration made the task of writing this book so much easier. There were, first of all, the Victor and Columbia phonograph companies, who placed at my disposal any and all popular music records that I required for my study and research; it was through these records, ever at my right hand in my home, that I was able to analyze and dissect our popular music with microscopic thoroughness. I am grateful to many of the musicians who are discussed in this book for going carefully through my manuscript, making valuable suggestions, and giving important advice. But for their co-operation, it is doubtful if I could have achieved accuracy and authority with a subject that is sadly obfuscated by press-agent legends.

CHAPTER ONE

KING OLIVER

"And That's How Ragtime Was Born . . . ."

KING OLIVER

♪

KING OLIVER

Nowhere else in America could ragtime have been born but in New Orleans. Shameless hussy that she was, ragtime—with her vitality, abandon, freedom from all inhibitions—fitted into the setting of vice as naturally as a diamond in platinum. She thrived in the fetid atmosphere of honky-tonks and brothels, for there she found not only a natural habitat but also her most ardent admirers. Later on, when she was to grow up as jazz and be considered for adoption by polite society, she would acquire the polish of respectability. Even then, however, this new respectability was to be mostly veneer; she never quite lost her New Orleans accent, that combination of incomparable independence, gusto, vitality, and earthiness.

It is worth noting that the temperament of ragtime *is* the temperament of New Orleans—a city recently described* as a "Marseille or a Shanghai, American style, shot through with the overtones of Christy Minstrels, a *code duello*, white steamboats on a chocolate-colored river, coffee and cotton, wine in cobwebbed bottles, vine-festooned patios, and Basin Street jazz. In a sense, she is the living heart of the Deep South." At the dawn of the present century, New Orleans was these things and many more. A blend of myriad per-

* Harold Sinclair, *The Port of New Orleans* (New York: Doubleday, Doran & Co., 1942).

sonalities and temperaments, New Orleans took to herself and absorbed the traits of her varied inhabitants: the warm blood and inflammability of spirit of the Spanish and the Creole, the voodoo superstition and restless dancing feet of the Negro, the freedom and tolerance of the Latin—all these became parts of her own character as well.

Her traditions had long been set. Soon after the purchase of Louisiana, the capital city began to swarm with gamblers, prostitutes, actors and actresses, gay cavaliers, drunkards, opium-smokers. Pleasure-seekers from the North came down the Mississippi on river boats for a rendezvous with pleasure in this gayest of all cities. Morality was, consequently, never kept to a rigid code. In 1857 the city licensed both brothels and their inmates, becoming the only city in America to legalize prostitution. In New Orleans' famed Storyville—center of pleasure and vice—there were brothels which were the last word in luxury: heavily carpeted and curtained, gleaming with crystal chandeliers, brass-inlaid furniture. And there were also shabby, shuttered, disease-laden one-room "cribs." The gambling houses, saloons, barrel houses likewise ran the gamut from ornate luxury to disheveled squalor. If anybody had been interested, he no doubt would have discovered that at one time or another in its history New Orleans contained more prostitutes than respectable women, more brothels than reputable business establishments, more saloons than schools and churches.

It was a free and easy city with an amazing tolerance toward all. The owner of a successful brothel was regarded with as much deference as the successful banker or doctor. Respectable parlors were crowded with gentlemen (their careers shady with questionable business affairs) paying genteel compliments to ladies of unblemished virtue. It was a gay city in which an illicit affair between a gentleman and a "quadroon" (fair-skinned daughter of a mulatto) was accepted casually. As a matter of fact, quadroons were raised by their mothers expressly to become mistresses of prosperous white men, to be consigned (at the dictate of tradition) to solitary womanhood when the men tired of them. It was a city in which good food and drink had been elevated to the status of a fine art, and good living became a golden rule. It was a city in which any novelty—whether a freak-show, a bullfight, a concert by a world-famous prima donna, or a prize match— would always find large and appreciative audiences.

Beyond all this, New Orleans was voodooism: in the swamps at the outskirts of the city the "tumultuous orgy would continue till the savage participants, entirely deprived of reason, fell to the ground from sheer lassitude, and were carried panting and gyrating into the open air."* New Orleans, finally, was the corybantic Saturday night dancing of the Negroes in Place Congo, where they would atavistically yield to the primitivism of the Bamboula, Counjai, or the Calinda.

2.

And that's where ragtime was born.

In that cradle of vice, dissipation, pleasure, and irresponsibility, ragtime was reared. It was an ungovernable child, shaped and formed by its environ-

* Marjorie B. Greenbie, *American Saga,* (New York: Whittlesey House, 1939).

ment. It was as much a part of New Orleans as Story-ville and the dances of Place Congo.

"Oh, you bitches, shake your asses," shouted the barber-turned-cornetist, Buddy Bolden, idol of Story-ville. Then, putting his lips to his cornet, he would produce a music full of strange impulses and emotional impacts. This music could not be found on any printed page, for it came from Buddy himself, deep within him, as natural a form of self-expression as his lewd vocabulary. Freddie Keppard would stick his head out of the window and strike up a demoniac chant on his trumpet till the crowds who gathered in the street to hear him went wild with excitement. Jelly Roll Morton would bang the piano in a cheap pleasure house, permitting his imagination to run amok in hours of improvisation on a simple theme.

They were completely unschooled—these troubadours of New Orleans. Most of them were unable to read a single note of music. They were guided only by instinct, by temperament, by their musical urges. They were the products of their background, and that background in turn found depiction in their music-making. And so they gave birth to a new musical style and idiom (not only in their composition but in their performance as well) the like of which could be heard nowhere else.

3.

All night long the blare of ragtime was heard in the pleasure domes of Storyville. In the smaller honky-tonks, the piano uttered a melancholy ragtime tune, one tune often serving as the entire repertoire for the pianist, but appearing in the many different guises of endless variations. Black men made fabulous music, whether with horns or with piano, to stir the blood and quicken the beat of the pulse.

But ragtime was not confined exclusively to Storyville. It was heard in the streets of New Orleans as well, as much a commonplace of everyday living there as great painting was in Renaissance Florence. During the day, Negro bands helped to publicize bargain sales, excursions, or theatrical performances. They contributed a decorative touch to the parades of lodges and secret societies. They accompanied funeral processions —in one direction, playing comparatively somber music; but on the way home, disgorging their ragtime to cheer up the mourners. Whatever the function or purpose for which these bands were employed, they would improvise music as they went. Sometimes it happened that two rival bands would meet in the street. Then and there a spirited competition would ensue to determine which of the bands had greater improvisational skill, or which one had the more inspired trumpeter or trombonist.

That so many of the best ragtime players were black-skinned points directly to the origin of this undisciplined music. It stemmed from the deepest sources of the Negro race: from the volcanic African rhythms which the Negro, in chains, had brought with him to the New World; from the plangent "sorrow songs" with which he bemoaned his fate in slavery; from the radiant spirituals with which he sought refuge in Christ and the promise of another happier world after this cruel existence; from the "shout"—his orgiastic absorption in religious worship—which was a throwback to his African ancestry.

After Emancipation, liberated Negroes flocked to New Orleans because it was a pleasure center, but more especially because its tolerant spirit extended even to those black of skin. In New Orleans, the Negro made music, as he had made music everywhere else, to express his deeply musical nature. He turned to wind instruments, partly because he realized that these instruments offered him a far richer medium for musical expression than the banjo, guitar, or human voice; partly because New Orleans had been the center for the manufacture of wind instruments for more than a century. Incapable of study, of application to the printed page, or of adherence to the accepted rule, the Negro learned to play these instruments by himself— and in his own way. Through endless experimentation, through trial and error, he created his own technique of performance, and with it strange and poignant effects, tone qualities, colors, as well as new harmonies based on a conscious, continuous deviation from pitch (things which no text could possibly teach him because it had never before existed). What the Negro actually was trying to do was to "sing" with his instrument, just as he had always given vent naturally and instinctively to song, whether at work, at play, or in prayer. Through the mouth of the cornet, trumpet, or trombone, he wished to *sing* his melancholy song and to reproduce the electrifying cry of the "shout." Thus he strove for a *vocal* style of performance rather than an *instrumental* one; and he achieved it through his own strange way of using *glissandi* and *vibrati,* with muted effects, all simulating the qualities of the singing voice. Hoarse and strident effects ("dirty" tone, it was later called) were as eagerly sought after as warm, fluid, singing quality. The Negro could not be discouraged by the limitations of his instrument for the simple reason that he had never been taught that it had any. Instead, through the employment of the most unorthodox means (the trombone technique of lip-slurring, the hanging of a derby on a trumpet for muting, the humming in the throat simultaneously with the sounding of a note on the trumpet to achieve a "growl") he arrived at new worlds of sound possibilities and tone colors. And a ragtime style was born.

It is possible to trace many of the elements which ragtime made its own—and by which it was henceforth to be identified—to the folk art which, over many years, the Negro had created in the South. Syncopated rhythms and shifting accents were found in spirituals, and particularly in the coonjine roustabout melodies with which Negroes accompanied their tasks of loading and unloading the Mississippi River boats; some of the coonjine melodies have about them an authentic ragtime flavor—and they had been sung more than fifty years before the official birth of ragtime. "Dirty" tone was a quality of singing which resulted from hours of orgiastic revelry and hysterical self-abandon in the religious "shouts." And the curious intonation created by sliding voices to tones foreign to the scale and to intervals smaller than the half-tone (yielding melodies and harmonies of exotic, almost barbaric, fascination) was found in Negro work songs, chain-gang songs particularly. Because these work songs had been sung out of doors, without the accompaniment of a musical instrument, they were perforce haphazard as to pitch and intonation; what began as a habit developed into a tradition.

The Negro could not read music. He was therefore compelled, in playing his instruments in New Orleans, to depend primarily on his own ingenuity and inventiveness for his music. It had always been so with the Negro. In the midst of a "shout" a new refrain would be sounded, one voice would interpolate a line, another voice would add a second line—and thus, spontaneously, a new Negro melody would come into being. In the fields at work, the leader might throw out a new phrase, and members of the gang would improvise a new work song, different laborers contributing different lines. In singing spirituals, the Negro had always permitted his imagination to play with the melody, frequently giving new shape and design to it. Improvisation was, indeed, second nature to the Negro musician.

Now, with horns to their lips, their imaginations would once again wander unhampered, soaring and expanding on wings of song. These players never used much more than the germ of a melodic idea, either of their own or another musician's creation. But, often at the inspiration of a moment, they developed and changed that idea as fancy dictated. These Negro players were driven by impulses they themselves could not understand or control—impulses which led them to embellish melodies with picturesque figurations, to venture upon long and fanciful cadenzas. They expanded a simple eight- or sixteen-bar subject like Scott Joplin's ever-popular *Maple Leaf Rag* with variations of seemingly inexhaustible fancy and performed it for hours at a stretch. They played as they felt. Out of these improvisations came a kind of dissonant counterpoint, as well as polyrhythm; and with them—though the music was generally crude and amorphous—came a wonderful feeling of spontaneity which, to this very day, has remained the most striking feature of every great "hot" jazz performance.

By evolving a new technique of performance and creating a new musical speech (from a vocabulary derived from their racial heritage) , the Negroes created ragtime. The name of ragtime was most probably derived from "ragging"—the clog-dancing of the Negroes. Ragtime has been described as syncopation in music— off-beat accents, continually suspended rhythms. But it is much more than a rhythmic device. It is a new musical language not only rhythmically but also in tone color, sequences, and harmonies. It is a Negroid music, and for this reason the Negro (with few exceptions) has been its happiest interpreter.

4.

Elsewhere in America, the favored popular music consisted of the sentimental ballads of Paul Dresser, Charles K. Harris, Stern and Marks, Harry von Tilzer, etc.: "My Mother Was a Lady," "After the Ball," "The Picture That I Turned to the Wall," "The Lost Child," "A Bird in a Gilded Cage." The 1890's was a sentimental period (and the period extended through the first few years of the twentieth century) , and it delighted in polite music, sentimentally extolling its high moral code, or weeping copious tears over the fate of any woman who lost her virtue. The melody was as lachrymose as the lyric.

But New Orleans, with its almost hysterical pursuit after pleasure, required sterner stuff than this. Out of that demand, and out of the spirit that was New Orleans, came the ragtime of the Negro. It could have come nowhere else. Only a febrile environment could have encouraged such a febrile musical expression. Besides, its vulgarity made it tabu even in some homes in New Orleans; how, then, could it be accepted and encouraged in cities more restrained? And, finally, no other city provided the Negro ragtime player with so many opportunities for employment. Other cities had their honky-tonks where such a musician might be welcome, but these were few and scattered. In New Orleans there were more than two hundred of them concentrated in one locality. It has been estimated that in ten years several hundred musicians found employment in Storyville. Negro musicians could also find employment by playing in parades in the streets, or in the parks; or they could get a job on the packet boats on the Mississippi River—some of New Orleans' best musicians served their apprenticeship on these boats, where they often combined their nighttime music-making with daytime functions as porter, barber, or waiter.

These dusky musicians were not well paid. They often tried to increase their meager earnings of about two dollars or so a night by passing the hat. But if they were not well paid in coin, their rewards in applause and adulation were handsome. In New Orleans the public made heroes of its favorite musicians. And like heroes, these musicians inspired legends. There was, for example, Buddy Bolden, of whom it was said that his tone on a still night could be heard for a distance of ten miles. They told the tale of the time when Buddy used to play at Johnson Park to large (and often hysterical) audiences. A competitor arose in John Robichaux of St. Louis, who had come to New Orleans and had taken his stand nearby at Lincoln Park, seducing Buddy's audiences away from him. Seeing himself without an audience (as terrifying to these musicians as it would have been for a respectable gentleman to find himself in the street without clothes), Buddy sounded his cornet and played. He played his favorites—pieces like the *Idaho Rag*—with all the skill and genius of which he was capable. His heart went into his playing as never before. Perhaps never again was he to play this way. In pairs, then in groups, finally in crowds, the people swarmed out of Lincoln Park and returned to listen to Buddy's wonderful music. "My chillun's come home," he remarked with quiet satisfaction.

There were other musical heroes in New Orleans besides the fabulous Buddy Bolden. But it was later generally accepted by those who knew their ragtime that of them all (Buddy not excluded) the king was Joe Oliver. Oliver's career resembles so closely the careers of all the other great ragtime men of New Orleans that to trace his history is to know the history of them all.

5.

He was born in New Orleans in 1885 and lived his childhood in the most abject poverty. The death of his mother, which occurred while he was still an infant, placed him under the care of a half-sister.

Like most New Orleans' men of music, Joe was fascinated by musical sounds early in life. He began playing the cornet and, because he had a genuine flair for it, was permitted to join a children's brass band which gave concerts in outlying districts. Later on in his life he earned his living as a butler, without neglecting his music. His employers recognized his love for music and sympathized with it to a point where they permitted him to send them a substitute butler whenever he had a musical engagement to fill.

Meanwhile, as Joe Oliver was growing up to manhood, ragtime was developed. He was twelve years old —it was in 1897—when the first ragtime smash hit, Kerry Mills' *Georgia Camp-Meetin'*, was published, and proved that ragtime had come to stay. Two years later Scott Joplin's *Maple Leaf Rag* came from St. Louis to take New Orleans by storm. At the same time there arose Negro players who could perform this music in the proper idiom: men like Buddy Bolden and Freddie Keppard, both of whom had risen to great popularity in the late 1890's.

Buddy Bolden was a model for imitation for all prospective ragtime players; and Joe Oliver was no exception. He studied Bolden's style, imitated it, then tried to improve it. He played in several bands, always experimenting with different styles of performance; from one of his first jobs he was summarily dismissed because he played too loud. Like all good ragtime players, he acquired his experience while barnstorming with small bands, working all the time on the crystallization of a style which was to become his own. At last he organized a band of his own. Now permitted to give his own manner free rein, he went to town. Before long his name was known throughout New Orleans.

Most Negro musicians of the time, once they had successfully established their reputations, sought employment in Storyville. So did Oliver. He held numerous minor jobs there without attracting much notice because Storyville seemed to have ears only for its own favorites—Bolden, Keppard, Perez. Undaunted, Oliver decided to prove his merits in a dramatic and decisive fashion. One day, while playing in a cabaret owned by the Aberdeen brothers, Joe instructed his pianist to sound the chord of B-flat. He began to play, seized by an inspiration which brought an altogether new quality to his tone. His pianist thumped out a steady beat as Oliver continued to play—his notes brilliantly articulated, his figurations free and fanciful. As he played, Joe marched across the cabaret floor and went out into the street. He directed his trumpet defiantly towards Pete Lala's house where Keppard and his Olympia Band were then playing, and performed a particularly difficult sequence with incomparable facility. Then, just as impudently, he directed another intricate phrase across the street where Emmanuel Perez was employed. And he continued playing. Before long, every gambling house, brothel, and honky-tonk in the neighborhood was emptied of its clientele. Like the Pied Piper, Joe played on as he turned about and re-entered the Aberdeen cabaret. And like the rats of Hamelin town, the habitués of Storyville followed him, electrified by this fabulous music-making.

After that they always spoke deferentially of Joe as

"King." He became the ace cornetist of Kid Ory's band (the top band in New Orleans) and had an army of disciples.

Like most ragtime players, Joe began to feel cramped and restricted in New Orleans once he had established his rule. He needed new worlds to conquer. The trend of musicians at that time was to go north to Chicago, where ragtime had begun to establish itself. Joe followed this trend in or about 1918.

As in New Orleans, so in Chicago: Oliver was a king. His introduction to Chicago took place in 1918 when he appeared with two different bands, one featured at Dreamland, the other at Royal Gardens. His virtuosity on the trumpet and his innate gift for improvisation found him numerous admirers. In 1920 Oliver formed a band of his own for Dreamland, soon to become nationally famous (following a successful tour) as King Oliver's Creole Jazz Band. After his tour Oliver returned to Chicago for a long engagement at the Lincoln Gardens. He was by this time hailed as the greatest trumpet performer of the day and one of the most brilliant ragtime improvisers.

Before long, however, he fell upon evil days. A series of misfortunes, beginning with a fire that destroyed the Lincoln Gardens, marked his decline. Indeed, some such unhappy destiny seemed to await most of the New Orleans musicians: Buddy Bolden went insane; Leon Rappolo, that fine clarinetist, became a marijuana addict and had to be confined in a sanitarium; Stale Bread—the spasm-band man—went blind. And Joe Oliver was no exception. After he had had a few tough breaks, he began to yield to fits of temperament and wounded pride. The King refused to admit the possibility that others might challenge his kingship: he must always be the top figure at any performance. His health deteriorated; pyorrhea robbed him of all his teeth so that he could no longer play his trumpet. Presently he was neglected—and then forgotten.

King Oliver's last years were pathetic. He was broke; he was nobody now. The few dollars he managed to pick up by working as a poolroom attendant were insufficient to pay for the medical treatment he needed. When in 1938 he died, he was given a decent funeral only because his sister provided the money for it; but there was no headstone to mark his grave—and there still is none.

Like most of the great New Orleans ragtime men of the past, Oliver is today little more than a name (if that) to jazz-lovers. A few records of his are still in existence, but those I have heard do not indicate the full extent of his powers as described and eulogized by those who heard him. But though his name, reputation, and even music died with him, his influence persists. He was one of the leading figures in that group of valiant troubadours of our popular music who helped create a new style of jazz performance, and to perfect and integrate it. Through his remarkable powers as a virtuoso, and through his gifts at ragtime improvisation, he helped establish ragtime as a vital and living force.

6.

The fall of the musical empire of New Orleans was at hand. Shortly after America entered the First World

War, Storyville was closed by an official ordinance of Secretary of the Navy Josephus Daniels. The brothels were closed; also the saloons, gambling houses, and honky-tonks. A veritable hegira of harlots and jazz musicians took place out of New Orleans. Actually, ragtime players had begun abandoning New Orleans for some time now: as the popularity of ragtime was being solidly established in Chicago, the call from the North for better musicians became more insistent. Since conditions in the North were far better for the musicians than they had been in the South—with more reasonable working hours and excellent pay—many of them followed the lead of Freddie Keppard. The closing of Storyville was therefore only the final process in a musical disintegration that had been taking place for some time.

And from New Orleans, the center of ragtime playing passed to Chicago.

CHAPTER TWO

♪

IRVING BERLIN

"The Melody Lingers On . . . ."

IRVING BERLIN

♪

IRVING BERLIN

Soon after ragtime had arisen in New Orleans, and long before it had developed into a definite idiom, it invaded New York. It arrived not in the form of authentic ragtime improvisation and instrumentation, but as syncopation. In 1896, at Tony Pastor's Theater, Ben Harney (who was to write a ragtime primer one year later) introduced "piano rag." In that year, too, Ernest Hogan wrote his classic "coon-song," "All Coons Look Alike to Me" (with special "rag" accompaniment), and a ragtime tune like "My Gal Is a Highborn Lady" became a nation-wide success.

Strictly speaking, these ragtime tunes, and the others which followed abundantly, were not New Orleans ragtime; they had merely appropriated one of its more superficial traits—that of the syncopated beat, the accent on the weak note instead of the strong one. They were almost as foreign to the genuine product that was developing in New Orleans as was the more formal tango that was also just coming in at this time. But by pointing a finger at ragtime, they suggested a rich new vein that could be tapped for popular song. And, by borrowing energetic rhythms, they injected the red blood of vitality into the veins of the then anemic song.

Though ragtime tunes had been known and liked throughout the country for more than a decade, ragtime did not become a national passion until a song called "Alexander's Ragtime Band" swept the country like a typhoon in 1911. Its composer was Irving Berlin, who only two years earlier had invaded Tin Pan Alley with his great talent and still greater ambitions. Berlin had showman blood in his veins. From his varied experiences as busker, singing waiter, and then vaudevillian, Berlin had learned to know his public. He realized that the overdose of sentimentality in song had begun to bore a large public. What the public now wanted was something galvanic, something better attuned to the increasing tempo and intensity of life. Berlin saw the answer in the ragtime tunes which had had varying success during the preceding decade. He decided that he, too, would write ragtime. And he wrote "Alexander's Ragtime Band," making popular-music history with it. In Tin Pan Alley it was a phenomenon, even though it followed a long series of ragtime melodies. "Alexander's Ragtime Band" was a phenomenon because it had its face toward the future, whereas all the successful Tin Pan Alley composers were looking only to the past—trying to imitate the formulas of yesterday's successes—concentrating on purely sentimental appeal.

Berlin's song, when introduced in Chicago by that dynamic vaudevillian Emma Carus in 1911, was immediately successful. "If we were John D. Rockefeller or the Bank of England," wrote one reviewer at this time, "we should engage the Coliseum, and get together a sextet including Caruso. . . . After the sextet sang it about ten times we should, as a finale, have Sousa's Band march about the building tearing the melody to pieces with all kinds of variations." Notwithstanding this enthusiasm, "Alexander's Ragtime Band" was turned down by Jesse Lasky for the Folies Bergère Theatre (now the Fulton) in New York. It therefore had its New York introduction at the Friars' Frolics in 1911, where it was sung by Berlin himself. Soon afterward it was featured in a burlesque show in New York called *The Merry Whirl*. Before long the public took to it, and it sold about a million copies.

Nor was this success ephemeral. In 1925 Carl Van Vechten wrote that, in his opinion, "Alexander's Ragtime Band" was "real American music—music of such vitality that it made the Grieg-Schumann-Wagner dilutions of MacDowell sound a little thin, and the saccharine bars of *Narcissus* and *Ophelia,* so much pseudo-Chaminade concocted in an American back-parlour, while it completely routed the so-called art music of the professors."* And many years after this, when the song was featured in a movie-cavalcade of Berlin hit-songs (for which it provided the title) , "Alexander's Ragtime Band" returned to score a decisive hit.

In its own day its influence was profound. Composers in Tin Pan Alley rubbed their eyes with incredulity and skepticism. Here was a song far removed from sentimental eyewash, and—miracle of miracles!—the public accepted it enthusiastically. Greater miracle still: the song had been written by a comparative newcomer! Almost inevitably there was envy, and then suspicion—the latter giving birth presently to the rumor that the song was not Berlin's, but that he had bought it from a Negro for ten dollars; and this tale actually gained wide credence for a while. (For many years, as Berlin followed this smash success with

* *Vanity Fair,* March, 1925.

numerous others, it was a standing joke among his friends that "the little Negro" was certainly supplying him generously with hit tunes.) But mean rumors could no more arrest the vogue of "Alexander's Ragtime Band" than Mrs. Partington could sweep away the incoming sea with her broom.

Even if, in the essentials of orchestration, improvisation, instrumental performance, harmony, and minutiae of rhythm, "Alexander's Ragtime Band" was not the genuine New Orleans ragtime, it had enough of ragtime's inherent abandon and animal spirits to give a new pulse and heartbeat to the effete popular music of the day. Numerous other ragtime tunes followed. Berlin himself wrote some half-dozen, including "Everybody's Doin' It," "International Rag," and "Ragtime Violin." Undisciplined, full of youthful energy (when compared to most of the songs that preceded them), these melodies delighted and invigorated the American public. Ragtime helped to heighten the countrywide craze for ballroom dancing, its syncopated rhythms stimulating restless feet. Finally, it gave an altogether new direction to the popular song, away from sentimentality and formulism, and toward an ever-increasing ingenuity of musical resources and intensity of moods. In that direction lay—jazz.

2.

Into the Tin Pan Alley of 1911 "Alexander's Ragtime Band" burst like a bombshell, completely disrupting an ordered world. Tin Pan Alley, America's street of song, was at the time on Twenty-eighth Street between Fifth and Sixth Avenues. It had originated in

Union Square where, in the gas-lit 1890's, the leading publishers and innumerable smaller ones clustered around the neighboring theaters, burlesques, garden restaurants, and saloons. In Union Square Tin Pan Alley acquired its tradition of manufacturing songs as if they were machine-made commodities; also that of publicizing them in the theaters and restaurants through the talents of the song-plugger. At the dawn of the century a general exodus of music publishers took place out of Union Square. They moved northward (following the uptown trend of hotels, theaters, and restaurants) until they congregated on Twenty-eighth Street. It was here that America's music industry acquired the picturesque sobriquet by which it was henceforth to be known—Tin Pan Alley, christened thus by an imaginative newspaperman.

It was Tin Pan Alley's pet credo that popular song hits were made, not born—pieced together through the effort of hard work and not through inspiration. Most of the composers were illiterate and dictated their tunes; virtually all of them wrote to set formulas. The great man of the Alley was not the composer of the song—of composers there was always an overabundance —but the song-plugger who brought it to fame. Upon his charm and personal appeal it depended whether the leading stars of the music hall, variety, or burlesque, the managers of cinema, restaurants, and theaters, would be persuaded to introduce a new number. His derby slightly askew, a cigar in his mouth, he would stand in the street outside the office that employed him, his eye alert for prominent producers or stars of the stage who might be passing by in search of songs. The song-plugger was often a performer in his own right, too, appearing as a part of a theatrical, cinema (song slides), or restaurant attraction; from his place in the audience, the limelight playing on him full force, he would collaborate in the performance of the songs he was pushing.

It was a smoothly functioning mechanism that Tin Pan Alley perfected. Different composers specialized in the writing of various standard types of songs, ranging from the "coon song" to the ballad; and these were turned out in wholesale quantities with factory-like precision. Once they were written, the song-plugger served as liaison between publisher and audience. But the Alley could operate efficiently only so long as its productions followed routine patterns of design and construction. Let a breath of originality enter—let one composer brush aside formulas to experiment with new styles and idioms—and the mechanism was clogged, production was disrupted. For machinery geared to mass production could not readily be converted to cope with growing complications.

"Alexander's Ragtime Band" was thus the first of a series of blows destined to break down the traditions established by Tin Pan Alley. Once these traditions were smashed, American popular songs were granted a new lease on life. The old Tin Pan Alley died with the emergence of Irving Berlin. A new Tin Pan Alley, placing emphasis on freshness, originality, and inspiration in song, rose, Phoenix-like, from the ashes of the old.

3.

The curious thing is that though Irving Berlin started the ragtime mania in America almost single-

handed, he was not (as has already been said) a ragtime composer. He was rather, we now know, a pioneer
in jazz—a word of which he had not even heard in 1911.
He was a transitional figure, bridging the gap between
the sentimental balladry and the coon songs of the
late 1890's and the early 1900's, and the mature jazz
of the 1920's. Of jazz much more will be written in
a later chapter. Here it is sufficient to point out that
Berlin was helping to evolve the new language of our
popular music by borrowing idioms and accents already in use, and enriching them with his imagination,
instincts, and creative gifts.

One of the truly fabulous figures in the history of
our popular music, Irving Berlin has been as influential as he has been popular. It is eloquently appropriate
that he who was destined to be one of its major creative
figures for more than three decades should have
ushered in a new age for popular music with one of
his early smash successes.

He was born as Israel Baline in Temun, a small
town in Siberia, on May 11, 1888. His only memory
of Russia was the sight of his home in flames as he lay
terrified, nearly concealed by a blanket. In 1892 the
Baline family was swept on the tide of the Jewish
migration from Russia and was carried with other
immigrants to the very heart of New York's East Side.
A large family, numbering eight children, the Balines
lived in poverty that could not be relieved by the
father's meager earnings as cantor in the synagogue
and as part-time supervisor of a *kosher* slaughter house.
But even such poverty seemed affluence when, in 1896,
the father died. To keep his family from actual starva-
tion, Israel—then aged eight—was forced to leave school

(he had never been much for book learning) and earn a living. For a while he sold newspapers in the streets. Having stemmed from a family which for generations had been cantors, it was perhaps, natural for him, before long, to try exploiting his voice. His father had frequently consoled himself with the thought that if his son Israel was never to become a Talmudic scholar, at least he could be a cantor, on the strength of a pleasing voice and a good ear.

Young Israel found a job leading through the streets of the Bowery a busker known as "Blind Sol," singing songs as he led him. Israel then became a busker himself, roving the streets of the Bowery and, with poignant soprano voice raised in the popular tunes of the day, encouraging charitable pennies. For a while he was engaged as a song-plugger in Tony Pastor's theater by the famous publisher-composer, Harry von Tilzer. In 1904 he got his first regular job, as singing waiter in Nigger Mike Salter's café in Pell Street, the first of several similar jobs.

Meanwhile, he began writing songs, turning to them as naturally as his ancestors had done, when, as cantors, they created their own religious cantillations. Long after the café in which he worked had been emptied of its clientele, Israel Baline would remain at his upright piano experimenting with original melodies. The story goes (it has been authenticated) that when Baline was singing in Salter's café, the waiter at Callahan's, a competing saloon nearby, had—in collaboration with Al Pianadozi—written and featured an Italian dialect song, "My Mariuch Take a Steamboat She Go Away." This song had gone over big with the clientele. Salter, piqued by the success of a competitor, spurred on his own singing waiters to emulation. One of them, Nick Michaelson, wrote the music, and Israel Baline provided the lyrics. It was called "Marie from Sunny Italy" and, published by Ted Snyder, it brought Baline his first revenue from song-writing—thirty-seven cents. On the printed sheet music appeared for the first time the name that posterity was to cherish—I. Berlin.

That little lyric converted Berlin into a song-writer. He wrote a second lyric about a Marathon runner named Dorando, on a ten-dollar commission by a vaudevillian. When the vaudevillian failed to call for his song, Berlin offered it to Snyder. "Of course, you have a melody for it?" Snyder said. Berlin said he did, although he had not even thought of one, and then and there improvised it. Snyder bought it for twenty-five dollars. In 1909 Berlin became staff lyrist for Ted Snyder, drawing twenty-five dollars a week charged against royalties. In 1910 he appeared in vaudeville, and, with that experience behind him, he acquired a singing part in a Shubert musical. But his heart was in composing. He wrote a series of humorous songs which (as one newspaper reported in 1910) "has set the country wild": "Sadie Salome, Go Home," which sold 300,000 copies; "My Wife's Gone to the Country," also approximately 300,000 copies; and "That Mesmerizing Mendelssohn Tune," 500,000 copies. Such substantial hits induced Snyder to take Berlin into partnership in his publishing firm. "Alexander's Ragtime Band" came in 1911—complete justification of Snyder's faith in the young composer. Less than two years after Berlin had first stepped foot into Tin Pan Alley, he was one of the top men of the profession.

Something of the impressive proportions of Irving

4.

Berlin's career is suggested by its span of more than three decades. But to appreciate more fully what he has achieved, let us look at some salient facts. Each of his first hits sold several hundred thousand copies, and "Alexander's Ragtime Band" reached the million mark; this was in 1910-1911. In 1942 the now rare phenomenon of a million-copy sale of a song recurred just when it seemed to have become a thing of the past —and it recurred with "White Christmas," which received the American Academy of Motion Pictures' award for the best song written in that year for a screen production.

During the first World War Berlin had surprised the country by organizing and writing an all-soldier show, *Yip-Yip-Yaphank,* with amateur material, scoring a decisive theatrical hit which brought thousands of dollars into the Camp Fund. And when in 1942 he announced another all-soldier show for the Second World War, the skeptics predicted that his luck would not strike twice. But Berlin answered them with *This Is the Army*—which, surpassing the success of his previous effort, earned several million dollars for various war efforts.

In 1938 he collaborated in the production of a film which was a tribute to his song-writing career—*Alexander's Ragtime Band,* a cavalcade of Berlin hit tunes over a period of several decades. In this same year a song he had discarded in 1917 was revived by him for Kate Smith, to become what some choose to speak of as our second national anthem, "God Bless America." In 1939 it was featured by the national presidential conventions of both major parties, and in 1940 it received the award of the National Committee of Music Appreciation for the best song of the year. Refusing to capitalize on patriotism, Berlin allocated all profits from that song—about a hundred thousand dollars—to the Boy and Girl Scouts.

By 1941—exactly thirty years after "Alexander"— Berlin was something of a musical laureate for the Government, commissioned to write songs for the Red Cross, for bond drives, for stimulating factory production, for the Navy Emergency Fund, for the President's Birthday Ball—and he continued to refuse any profits from such work. In 1943 he was deservedly honored with a citation by the National Association for American Composers and Conductors as "the outstanding composer of popular music."

Unquestionably, Irving Berlin's prime achievement —and one for which there is hardly a parallel—has been his ability to produce successful songs for over three decades, year in and year out, his best earning high rank (if not indeed the highest) among each year's successes. This becomes the more remarkable when we consider the limitations under which he works. For no sound musical background nurtured his imagination, no thorough technical equipment has facilitated for him the task of translating musical ideas into form and substance. His knowledge of harmony, theory, form, counterpoint is less than what may be found in an elementary textbook. He can play the piano in only one key, his keyboard having a special mechanism which, by a flip of the lever, enables him to play in this key. For setting his melodies on paper, he must depend on a musical secretary. He has virtually no acquaintance with musical literature, and is not likely to be encountered at Carnegie Hall. Altogether he is—and he makes no effort to conceal the fact—a musical ignoramus. Yet he is, despite all this, one of our most brilliantly endowed and richly productive composers, and undeniably one of the most important.

To an interviewer he has confided his *modus operandi:* "I usually get a phrase first. . . . 'Berlin's hat is on his desk.' There's a phrase that might hit me. I keep repeating it over and over, and the first thing I know I begin to get a sort of rhythm, then a tune. I don't say all my songs are written that way, for sometimes I hear a tune first and then start trying to fit words to it. In either case, whichever part comes first serves as a mold into which the other part must be poured."*

With instinct and taste—and with a melodic inventiveness that now appears inexhaustible—he has produced almost a thousand songs to lyrics of his own creation. A large number of these, it is true, are overstylized, too enslaved to a convenient formula to be completely acceptable. But the best of them have a stamp of their own which no one else seems able to counterfeit successfully. His richest vein is that of exquisite tenderness, sentiment without sentimentality. To lyrics expressing self-pity, he has fashioned melodies of stabbing beauty, poignancy; though their emotional range is not wide, they are effective. But it should be emphasized that Berlin is too richly gifted a composer to strum one string alone; this is doubtless one of the secrets of his sustained success. He has written numbers like "Alexander's Ragtime Band," "Heat

* S. J. Woolf, "What Makes a Song: A Talk with Irving Berlin," *New York Times* Magazine, July 28, 1940.

Wave," "I Love a Piano," and "Pack Up Your Sins," which depend for their effectiveness not upon an emotional melody but on rhythmic ingenuity and cleverly shifting accents. He has written mildly humorous ditties like "Oh, How I Hate to Get Up in the Morning," "My Wife's Gone to the Country," "This Is the Life," and "They Call It Dancing," which are deft.

But his most unforgettable moments are those in which the softness of his expression, the sensitivity of his mood, the refinement and grace of his style are reminiscent of the song styles of the great composers of *Lieder*, though of course, their artistic scope is much more limited. In songs like "Always," "What'll I Do?" "Remember," "Cheek to Cheek," "Blue Skies," he achieves undisputed greatness as a writer of melody. George Gershwin, who need envy no man's melodic talent, once spoke of Berlin in the following manner: "Irving Berlin is the greatest American song composer. He has vitality, both rhythmic and melodic, which never seems to lose its freshness. He has that rich, colorful melodic flow which is ever the wonder of those of us who, too, compose songs. His ideas are endless. His songs are exquisite cameos of perfection. Each one of them is as beautiful as its neighbor. Irving Berlin is America's Franz Schubert."

Another great popular composer, Jerome Kern, expressed his admiration of Berlin no less impressively: "Berlin, like Wagner, an inexorable autocrat, molds and blends and ornaments his words and music at one and the same time, each being the outgrowth of the other. He trims and changes and refashions many times, but nearly always strives for simplicity, never elaboration. He is not bothering much with the seats of the Olympians, but he is concerned with the lore, the hearts—yes, and the dancing feet—of human folk. The comparison between the craft of Wagner and Berlin is not a heedless one. . . . There are phrases in Berlin's music as noble and mighty as any clause in the works of the masters from Beethoven and Wagner down."*

5.

The economic holocaust of 1929 swept away Irving Berlin's fortune. For the first time in his life, he knew panic. Since "Alexander's Ragtime Band" his economic position had been so secure that he had never had to worry seriously about money. By 1912 he was earning a handsome income from song royalties, music-hall appearances in London, and from his partnership in the publishing house of Waterson, Snyder & Berlin, Inc. Ten years later his income swelled to several times that figure. In 1916 he wrote his first complete score for Broadway, *Watch Your Step*—the beginning of a long and profitable association with the theater. In 1919 he undertook a vaudeville tour which alone netted him two thousand dollars a week, and founded the publishing house of Irving Berlin, Inc., which from the first was a successful venture—as any publishing establishment was predestined to be if it had the exclusive rights to the songs of Irving Berlin! He wrote scores for the *Ziegfeld Follies* of 1918, 1919, and 1920, producing such outstanding hits as "Say It With Music," "A Pretty Girl Is Like a Melody," and

* Alexander Woollcott, *The Story of Irving Berlin* (New York: G. P. Putnam's Sons, 1925).

"Mandy." And, in 1921, he and Sam H. Harris built the highly successful Music Box Theater, one of the soundest theatrical investments on Broadway. There, for a few years, he helped to produce and composed all the music for the annual *Music Box Revue,* which brought substantial revenue into the box office. In 1926 he entered the Social Register with his marriage to Ellin Mackay, daughter of the owner of Postal Telegraph.

Then, suddenly, in 1929, Berlin's wealth collapsed like a house of cards. His personal fortune gone, nothing remained—except his great talent. Now, for the first time in almost twenty years, he must depend entirely on composition for a livelihood. For a while he was seized with terror. Perhaps he had lost that touch? Perhaps it was no longer possible for him to produce successes—now that he needed them so badly? Perhaps his best work was definitely behind him? Perhaps his public had grown tired of him? Perhaps this financial pressure would choke his creative vein?

But it was soon evident that these fears were baseless, that Berlin's fertility was as rich as ever. He was still the master of his art, still peerless in the writing of tender, seductive tunes of incomparable enchantment. In *Face the Music* (1931), *As Thousands Cheer* (1932), and *Louisiana Purchase* (1940) he brought to Broadway the most successful musical shows of their respective seasons. In Hollywood he wrote a series of effective scores for the films, including *Top Hat* (which alone netted him $300,000), *Follow the Fleet,* and *Holiday Inn* (all three for Fred Astaire), *Carefree, Second Fiddle, Louisiana Purchase,* and *This Is the Army.*

♪

CHAPTER THREE

Louis Armstrong

"Chicago, Chicago, That's Where I Belong . . . ."

LOUIS ARMSTRONG

♪

LOUIS ARMSTRONG

It was in Chicago that the word "jazz" (or "jaz" as it was sometimes spelled at first) came into general usage. On October 27, 1916, *Variety* commented as follows: "Chicago has added another innovation to its list of discoveries in the so-called 'jazz bands.' The jazz band is composed of three or more instruments and seldom plays regulated music. The College Inn and practically all the other high-class places of entertainment have a jazz band featured, while the low cost makes it possible for all smaller places to carry their jazz orchestras.

Where had the word come from? Its etymological origin has inspired some controversy and a great deal of speculation. Was it derived from the French word *jaser*—meaning "to chatter" or "to prattle"; or did it come from the minstrel show term "jasbo"? Some believe it came from Creole patois. Others suspect that a Negro musician in New Orleans may have been named Charles or James and that the word jazz might have arisen from the contraction of his name to "Chas." or "Jas." ("Let's have some more of that music, Chas.!"). In the language of the gutter it had a definite sexual connotation. In theaters it was used by actors as a synonym for pep or excitement.

Whatever its origin, we may be reasonably certain that the word was never officially used to describe popular music in New Orleans. It emerged in Chicago soon after the great northward flight of ragtime players which converted the city of smoke and steel into a ragtime center in succession to New Orleans.

As early as 1908 Jelly Roll Morton, ragtime pianist and composer, had come to Chicago to work at the Elite. But the official introduction of New Orleans ragtime to Chicago came in 1914. In that year a vaudevillian named Gorham visited New Orleans. During his strolls in the streets he came upon a group of four white New Orleans ragtime players advertising a prizefight. The music held him spellbound. He learned from the leader of this group (a fellow by the name of Brown) that not a single player could read a note of music, and that their playing was for the most part a spontaneous eruption. Gorham at once recognized the showman value of this ensemble. When he returned to Chicago he decided to import it. Now called the Brown Band from Dixieland, it was placed in Lamb's Café where, featuring the *Livery Stable Blues*, it took the town by storm.

Brown's success sent other cafés in Chicago scurrying for New Orleans bands of their own. To the Boosters' Club at the Hotel Morrison and to the Schiller Café came the Original Dixieland Band. It was with this group that, it is now believed, the word "jazz" made its appearance. The story goes (Nicolas Slonimsky has authenticated it by direct correspondence with original sources*) that while this group was performing at the Boosters' Club, one of the dancing couples kept calling for "more jazz." The persistence with which the couple kept referring to the music as "jazz" in-

---

* Nicolas Slonimsky, *Music Since 1900* (New York: W. W. Norton & Co., 1937).

spired the manager of the band to rename his group the Original Dixieland Jazz Band. Tom Brown, too, added "Jazz" to the name of his organization.

By 1917 the word was in general usage by most of the leading ragtime bands in Chicago. As *Variety* noted on January 5, 1917: "The most popular attractions in Chicago cabarets are the jaz bands or orchestras, and every cabaret, regardless of its size, has a jaz aggregation." In March of the same year Victor issued its first jazz record, a release by the Original Dixieland Jazz Band of *Livery Stable Blues,* coupled with *Dixieland Jazzband One-Step*. Dixieland recordings eventually sold millions of copies.

2.

But jazz was then merely a more official and popular name for the ragtime music of the New Orleans troubadours. Ragtime in New Orleans, jazz in Chicago —a rose by any other name. . . . When Storyville closed during the first World War, the leading ragtime performers came to Chicago in increasing numbers, enticed by the great success of their predecessors and by the realization that in Chicago working conditions and pay were far better than they had been in New Orleans. Sidney Bechet had brought his clarinet to the De Luxe Café in 1916. Freddie Keppard came in 1917. He was followed by King Oliver and Johnny Dodds; also by Leon Rapollo and Paul Mares, who were to become the nucleus of the New Orleans Rhythm Kings.

It was during his engagement at the Lincoln Gardens

that Oliver sent a call to New Orleans for his protégé (also a trumpet virtuoso) to join him. In 1922 Louis Armstrong, then twenty-two years old, came north to add his trumpet to that of the King. Together they made music the like of which—so they said—Chicago could hear nowhere else. They inspired each other, magnetized each other, encouraged in each other unparalleled flights of musical fancy. Without resorting to any printed music, without even looking at each other, they synchronized as no two jazz trumpets could elsewhere, understanding each other through what appeared to be infallible instinct. They went through a "break" with stunning virtuosity and with a beautiful sense of co-ordination which took away the breath of those who heard them.

His collaboration with young Louis Armstrong marked King Oliver at the height of his fame and powers. In 1924 Armstrong left Oliver to work out his own destiny.

3.

Louis Armstrong was born in New Orleans on July 4, 1900. He was innately musical. As a boy he enjoyed nothing more than to visit the Mississippi docks with his friends and there spend hours in singing. He soon formed a boys' vocal quartet which would roam the streets singing the hot tunes of the day and collecting charitable pennies and nickels. The quartet performed in the streets and honky-tonks of Storyville, where its members were introduced not only to some of the shadier aspects of night life, but also to the great ragtime-playing of men like Buddy Bolden. In 1913, because he permitted his New Year's Eve exuberance to express itself in the firing of a gun in the street, Armstrong was confined for a year to the Waifs' Home. That confinement proved providential, for it was there that Armstrong became a trained musician. A sympathetic keeper, named Peter Davis, recognized in him signs of musical gift and taught him the trumpet. Louis played in the Waifs' Home Band, eventually becoming its leader.

He left the Waifs' Home in his fourteenth year, already quite agile in his use of the trumpet, and already famed for his formidable lung power. Still too young to join a band, he sold papers in the streets, then found a regular job in a dairy—satisfying his musical urges only intermittently by taking an occasional assignment in Storyville's gin mills for a dollar a night.

In his seventeenth year he came directly under the influence of King Oliver, to whose trumpet-playing with Kid Ory's Band he had been an indefatigable auditor. To him, Oliver was a hero for worship and imitation. Determined to come more intimately into contact with his idol, Armstrong befriended Oliver's wife, ran errands for her and, at last, was given opportunity to come into the hallowed presence of the king. Oliver was as much flattered by the boy's adulation as he was impressed by his sincerity. He took Louis under his personal wing, taught him some of the tricks of handling a trumpet and improvising a ragtime "break." Oliver's interest inevitably attracted Armstrong to the attention of ragtime players, who now called on him more and more frequently for random assignments.

When he was seventeen (not long after he had come under Oliver's influence), Armstrong formed his own band and, as was to be expected, modeled it directly after Kid Ory's. This proved invaluable experience in preparing him for the major assignment that now called to him. King Oliver went on to greener pastures in Chicago. The vacancy in Kid Ory's band, on Oliver's recommendation, was given to Armstrong.

An unhappy early marriage led him to leave New Orleans. He found the opportunity in an offer from Fate Marable to join his band on the Mississippi excursion boat *Dixie Belle*. These excursion boats, which during the spring and summer traveled as far north as St. Louis and St. Paul, and in the winter roamed around New Orleans and other river towns, heard some of the best ragtime music in the country. For two years (and approximately five thousand miles) Armstrong's trumpet contributed to the joyous music-making. It was, as Armstrong himself realized, useful experience. "I could read music very well by now and was getting hotter and hotter on my trumpet. My chest had filled out deeper and my lips and jaws had got stronger, so I could blow much harder and longer than before without getting tired. I had made a special point of the high register, and was beginning to make my high-C, and more often."*

In 1922 a telegram arrived from King Oliver urging Armstrong to join his band.

* Louis Armstrong, *Swing That Music* (New York: Longmans, Green & Co., 1936).

4.

When Armstrong came to Chicago it was already well on its way toward being the capital of jazz. Postwar hysteria, disillusionment, live-today-for-tomorrow-we-die philosophy found expression in the hyperthyroid music of ragtime. Chicago provided a haven for the jazz artist because—city of bootleggers and racketeers—it had more night spots demanding such music than any other city in the country. It was a city of many personalities, and the personality to which hot music had the greatest appeal was the tough one of vice and corruption.

But Chicago became the capital of jazz not only because it absorbed into itself many of the greatest of New Orleans' ragtime artists, but also because it was capable of creating a school of its own. Why it was that there should have developed in Chicago, and Chicago alone, so many fine jazz artists—and in one period— has, no doubt, a variety of explanations. There were the incomparable masters of New Orleans there to set an example and to tempt emulation—men whose personal magnetism and extraordinary native powers inevitably exerted a profound influence on younger men. There was Chicago's night life, where money and bootlegged liquor flowed so freely, offering opportunities for the exploitation of these performers. Besides café and night spots there were small rooms, open when all others were closed, where musicians would gather to practice their art for their own and each other's gratification.

There was the band called the Wolverines, third of the great white jazz bands in succession to the Original

Dixieland Jazz Band and the New Orleans Rhythm Kings. One of the greatest virtuosos of the Wolverines was the fabulous "Bix" Beiderbecke, perhaps the greatest of all jazz cornetists. Bix had never taken a cornet lesson, but had acquired his musical education by listening to the family phonograph and imitating the style and tricks of La Rocca and Oliver. In 1923, after jobbing around in Chicago and on excursion boats with several different bands, Bix helped to organize the Wolverines. It was his artistry which helped to make this one of Chicago's greatest ensembles. His style had greater artistic refinement and restraint than that of Oliver, and he helped to bring to his ensemble subtle tints and shades of which other bands were temperamentally incapable. Through the texture of his ragtime band, the notes of his cornet sounded full and clear, recognizable for his beautiful phrasing, his suave legato, his luxurious tone, particularly in the middle register. Of Chicago's jazz performers, *he* was the artist (his musical tastes, outside of jazz, included the music of Stravinsky, Ravel, and Debussy). In his lifetime—which was brought to a premature end by overindulgence in liquor—he was generally spoken of as one of the greatest of jazz men. It is not difficult to understand why, for his recordings reveal the full stature of his artistry. Since his death in 1931, he has become something of a legend in jazz circles, recognizably the inspiration and central figure of a bestselling novel, Dorothy Baker's *Young Man with a Horn*.

There was also the Austin High School band, a group of jazz-crazy kids, which gave to popular music such men as Jimmy MacPartland (cornetist), Frank

Teschmaker (clarinetist), and Bud Freeman (saxophonist). The youngsters were inspired by a jukebox to which they listened tirelessly in an ice-cream parlor near their school. The record they preferred was one played by the New Orleans Rhythm Kings, and to this they would listen again and again until they felt they had assimilated the most detailed mannerisms of the ensemble. At about this same period they heard King Oliver's band, which proved to be a second great influence. The Austin High School boys called themselves the Blue Friars and played, with extraordinary verve and freshness, in a variety of night spots and dives. Eventually, members of the Austin High School group were absorbed by the Wolverines, but not before their influence had been felt and absorbed by other Chicago jazz groups.

Within the span of a few years following the emergence of the Wolverines and the Austin High School band, the night spots of Chicago's broad avenues and somber alleys produced great jazz men in what appeared to be unceasing numbers: guitarist Eddie Condon, pianists Earl Hines and Jess Stacey, drummer Gene Krupa, cornetist "Muggsy" Spanier, and clarinetist Benny Goodman. It was a big parade of jazz artistry the like of which has yet to be duplicated.

5.

In such an atmosphere, saturated with jazz playing and jazz music of the highest order, Louis Armstrong rose to heights. His style was gaudier than that of Beiderbecke, whose discipline and refinement were far removed from Armstrong's headstrong temperament.

Essentially a showman who gloried in the limelight, Armstrong went in for display both in his performance on the trumpet and in his stage behavior. His exhibitionism—revealed in gestures like the smacking of his lips on the trumpet, or cavorting on the stage—finds a counterpart in his delight in virtuosity for its own sake: those dazzling succession of high-C's, that indulgence in ear-splitting sonorities, that glittering array of *glissandi*. But though his playing is given to meretricious display, its power and inventiveness can never be questioned. Today in New York, as yesterday in Chicago, he is still the first in the line of great jazz trumpets. In selecting an All-American Band for *Esquire* in 1934, the Belgian hot-jazz expert, Robert Goffin, wrote: "Concerning the selection of Louis Armstrong as trumpeter on the 'first team' of the All-American Band there can be . . . no dispute. He *made* jazz and is the true king of jazz. Anyone who knows anything about the subject will concede this." As a matter of fact, Goffin opened his article with the following words: "To begin with, it's very simple. Opposite the place where it says 'trumpet' you merely set down the name of Louis Armstrong."*

He is both an outstanding technician and a stylist. He has exuberance and gusto which exhaust his listeners, and intensity and deep feeling. His tone is one of luxuriant beauty, warm, rich, intoxicating. His imagination in improvisation is fertile. He is, indeed, as Virgil Thomson once wrote somewhere in a rhapsodic moment, a "master of musical art comparable only . . . to the great *castrati* of the eighteenth century. His style of improvisation would seem to have combined

* "Esquire's All-American Band," *Esquire*, February, 1943.

the highest reaches of instrumental virtuosity with the most tensely disciplined melodic structure and the most spontaneous emotional expression, all of which in one man you must admit is pretty rare."

In Chicago not only his trumpet virtuosity reached its fullest development, but also his unique style of vocal delivery. His singing, undoubtedly a throwback to the religious "shouts" of the southern Negroes, is as much a characteristic of his jazz art as his brilliant trumpet-playing, and is in a measure influenced by it. That guttural shout of his, with an eloquence of its own, is an integral part of his personality as a jazz artist.

In 1924 Armstrong married the brilliant jazz pianist Lillian Hardin. It was Lil who encouraged him to abandon Oliver's outfit and to set out for himself. For a brief period Armstrong went to New York to join the famous jazz orchestra of Fletcher Henderson, which was appearing at Roseland. But he was not happy with Henderson. Henderson's orchestra was the first colored ensemble to depend upon elaborate orchestrations; obedience to the printed page was demanded. In following music by note, Armstrong felt himself musically smothered. He was meant to soar on the wings of his imagination. He returned to Chicago to join the jazz band organized for the Dreamland Café by his wife. Back in Chicago, and in the arms of real jazz, he felt as though he had left prison walls for the open air of freedom.

For the next few years Armstrong enjoyed that adulation in Chicago which few jazz men—King Oliver not excluded—knew. His appearances at the Dreamland Café, Vendome Theater, and the Savoy brought him to the very pinnacle of his fame.

6.

As was the case with New Orleans, so was it to be with Chicago. The period of jazz glory, brilliant though it was, was destined for eclipse. Toward the close of the 1920's, Chicago's great era of early jazz drew to a close. A new hegira had begun—this time to New York. Chicago was being sucked dry of its jazz artists. The new capital was New York.

Louis Armstrong joined this parade eastward in 1929. Geographic change did not in any way temper his success, or his capacity to magnetize his public. Under the managerial wing of Joseph G. Glaser—his first and, up to the present time, his only personal manager—Armstrong retained his regal position in the world of hot jazz. He appeared in the Savoy Ballroom in Harlem, at Connie's Inn, and in other famous night clubs, duplicating one triumph after another. In the Broadway revue *Hot Chocolates,* in a series of talking pictures starring Bing Crosby, Mae West, Jack Benny, and Dick Powell, and in his radio broadcasts over the Columbia network, Armstrong continued to dominate the world of jazz with his magnificent trumpet-playing.

Not only has he made a highly successful transcontinental tour, but he has several times taken his trumpet to Europe. There he has played before royalty— the Prince of Wales and the Duke of York (as they then were), the Crown Princess of Italy, and many other notables in Paris, Brussels, Vienna, Geneva, and Copenhagen. When Louis Armstrong puts his trumpet to his lips and lets his musical imagination wander, he speaks to royalty as an equal. For he, too, is a king.

CHAPTER FOUR

W. C. HANDY
MEADE LUX LEWIS

"Got Dem Blues, But I'm
Too Damned Mean To Cry . . . ."

W. C. HANDY

♪

W. C. HANDY

To the texture of what soon was to be known as jazz
had been added the element of ragtime. Other elements
in harmonic and melodic color and in tonality were
to be contributed by the blues of W. C. Handy. For
years before Handy wrote his classics, "The Memphis
Blues" and the "St. Louis Blues," music similar in
general character to the later blues had been in existence. But it was Handy who stylized its form, gave it
nationwide recognition, and established it permanently.

The blues was, after all, the "sorrow music" of the
lower strata of Negro society—gamblers, prisoners,
prostitutes, beggars, shifting laborers. It was the deep-
throated lament of those harassed people bewailing
their misfortunes. The blues was the simple, poignant
cry of woe, and it was fraught with the profoundest
feelings. With Handy, its elementary structure—as
simple as the nature of the people who sang it—made
it easy to remember. One line was repeated, then a
new line was added to complete a three-line stanza, in
the following manner.

> I had been a bad, bad girl, wouldn' treat nobody right,
> I had been a bad, bad girl, wouldn' treat nobody right,
> They want to give me thirty-five years, someone wanted
>   to take my life.
>
> Judge, please don' kill me, I won't be bad no' mo'—
> Judge, please don' kill me, I won't be bad no' mo'—
> I'll listen to ev'ybody, something I never done befo'.

The musical construction was equally simple. The melody was usually of twelve-bar length, with three equal phrases of four bars each. Certain technical features, now accepted as essentials of blues structure, were early established by Handy: the freedom of the rhythm; the alternation from major to minor and vice-versa; the unique intonation based upon an emphasis on the third and seventh notes of the major scale; the individual harmony arising from a repeated use of the dominant seventh chord.

In elaborating on the technique he adopted for his own gems, Handy has also indirectly thrown illumination on the style and idiom of all accepted blues: "The primitive Southern Negro as he sang was sure to bear down on the third and seventh tone of the scale, slurring between major and minor. Whether in the cotton field of the Delta or on the levee up St. Louis way, it was always the same. Till then, however, I had never heard this slur used by a more sophisticated Negro, or by any white man. I had tried to convey this effect in 'Memphis Blues' by introducing flat thirds and sevenths (now called blue notes) into my song, although its prevailing key was major; and I carried this device into my melody as well. I also struck on the idea of using dominant seventh as opening chord of the verse of the 'St. Louis Blues.' This was a distinct departure, but as it turned out, it touched the spot.

"In the folk blues the singer fills up occasional gaps with words like 'Oh Lawdy,' or 'Oh, Baby!' and the like. This meant that in writing a melody to be sung in the blues manner, one would have to provide gaps or waits. In my composition I decided to embellish the piano and orchestra score at these points. This kind of business is called a 'break' . . . and 'breaks' became a fertile source of the orchestral improvisation which became the essence of jazz. In the chorus of 'St. Louis Blues' I used a plagal chord to give 'spiritual' effects in the harmony. Altogether I aimed to use all that is characteristic of the Negro from Africa to Alabama."[*]

The blues was half-brother to the spiritual, for both had their origins in the compulsion of a musical people to express the tragedy of its fate. The spiritual was the Negro's escape into religion, and was sung by groups. The blues—the Negro's awareness of his trials and frustrations on earth—was a lonely man's lament, and was sung by a single voice. The songs of the spirituals were of Jesus and Heaven; those of the blues were of earthly realities, of the dreary events and experiences in an everyday world. "De blues ain't nothing! No, de blues ain't nothin', but a good man feelin' blue," is the refrain of an early blues heard in honky-tonks in the Southwest. Good men feeling blue, singing intensely of their feeling, gave birth to the blues. It was an emotional outlet. There is a good deal of astuteness in the observation made by Hugues Panassie that "when the Negro sings the blues it is not to give way to his sadness but to free himself of it."[†]

Soon after the Civil War, many of the emancipated Negroes turned to music for a livelihood, playing their guitars or banjos, and singing their tunes on street corners, in bawdy houses, and in saloons. They sang various types of song; but the one that came most naturally to them was that which reflected their usu-

* W. C. Handy, *Father of the Blues: An Autobiography*, edited by Arna Bontemps (New York: The Macmillan Co., 1941) .
† Hughes Panassie, *The Real Jazz* (New York: Smith & Durrell, 1942) .

ally somber moods. These musicians might travel from town to town (frequently alone) singing their laments, often with improvised words. Some of these troubadours had no other occupation but to make music all night; during the day they slept. Others would supplement the income from an occasional job with the pennies and nickels earned from public performances. These musicians found employment in the lowest dives of the South and the Southwest, in the North and Northwest, singing their sad tunes in Memphis' Beale Street, in New Orleans, or on the levees of St. Louis.

The early Negro lamentations moaned over many things: tornadoes, storms, hard times, cruelty, the coldness of a loved one, racial oppression, prisons, boll weevils. Similar subjects—and others like Joe Turner, the white officer who (like the personification of an implacable Fate) would come to Memphis to carry off handcuffed Negroes to Nashville for prison sentences—were exploited for the blues. The blues were elemental. Their crudity was that of the Negro "shout," with its primitive emotion and intense speech. But their mood and poignant expression were those of the "sorrow song" in which the tragedy of an oppressed people is voiced in unforgettable accents.

2.

It was W. C. Handy who gave the blues its name, and who popularized the form it was henceforth to know.

Born in Florence, Alabama, on November 16, 1873,

William Christopher Handy was the son of a pastor who considered the practice of music the devil's pastime. Young William was innately musical, giving signs of his musical nature in ways more pronounced than a pair of large ears to which his grandmother always pointed with pride as proof that the boy was a born musician. His musical urges, however, had to be stifled, or given a secret outlet. Once, at school, he confessed to his teacher that it was his ambition to become a professional musician. The teacher, shocked, gave him a severe lecture and sent a note of protest to his father. "Son," Father Handy said to the boy, "I'd rather see you in a hearse than have you a musician!" On another occasion, when his father discovered that William had secretly bought a guitar (with pennies he had saved over a period of many months from earnings at any and every job that presented itself), he insisted that the boy return the instrument and take in exchange a copy of Webster's Unabridged Dictionary.

A trumpeter from Birmingham, who had come to play with the local Baptist choir, inspired in the boy the desire to play the instrument. William fashioned one out of a cow's horn, which provided scant satisfaction to a boy with music in him crying for an outlet. Finally, he bought a trumpet from a visiting circus musician for one dollar (twenty-five cents cash, the remainder paid in installments). Handy practiced diligently, and in great secrecy. It was not long before he became a member of a band. Neither the hickory stick nor the stern disapproval of his father could keep him from his appointed mission. He joined a minstrel show and went on tour with it. The show was left stranded on the road, and Handy was compelled to jump rides on freight trains for his passage home.

That experience may have convinced him, temporarily at any rate, that the life of a musician was too precarious for comfort. He decided to become a teacher. He passed the necessary examination in Birmingham, but when he learned that his salary would be less than that of an ordinary day laborer, he abandoned the thought of teaching and became a foundry hand.

But music was too strong a compulsion to be permanently abandoned. Handy combined foundry work with organizing and directing a brass band. Then—when the panic during Cleveland's second administration closed many factories throughout the country—Handy returned to music professionally. For the next few years his was a nomadic existence. He came to St. Louis and, unable to find employment, slept for a week on the levee, penniless and hungry. He heard the strange, soft strains of songs with which Negro hands at the docks lightened their tasks, songs which impressed themselves permanently on his memory. As they worked, and as they sang, Handy thought of his old driving ambition. He became more determined than ever to devote himself entirely to the making of music.

His was a trying existence. Musical jobs were not plentiful, and those that turned up paid poorly. But, in 1896, a permanent musical post brought an end to destitution. He was engaged as cornetist for Mahara's Minstrels, combining the playing of the cornet with the preparation of orchestral arrangements and with personal appearances with a quartet in the "olio."

Eventually, when the minstrels carried two bands, Handy was assigned to lead one of them.

Handy remained with Mahara's Minstrels until 1903 except for a brief interval in 1900 when he served as teacher of music in a small agricultural college. For a period he led the colored Knights of Pythias Band in Clarksdale, Mississippi.

It was at this time that he heard a lonely Negro sing one of the laments of his race at a deserted railroad station. As he listened to this poignant singing, Handy knew that he had undergone a profound musical experience. What he could not realize at the time was that this experience was ultimately to shape his musical future; for the singing of that Negro was one of several important influences that were to bring Handy to the writing of his blues.

3.

The hearing of the Negro song was, however, only one of several steps in the education of W. C. Handy, and in his development as a composer. The second of his great experiences took place soon afterward, when he and his band performed in Cleveland, Mississippi. He was asked to play some "native" music and, not understanding the request, he played a Southern melody. What was really wanted was a slow drag. A second request succeeded the first: Would Handy object if a band of local colored musicians performed a few numbers?

The enthusiasm with which this music was greeted— dollars, half-dollars, quarters were showered on the musicians by the appreciative audience—brought to Handy the realization that there was something vital in this popular music, something which made a direct appeal to masses and which could not be neglected. "They had the stuff people wanted," he wrote in his autobiography. "It touched the spot. Their music wanted polishing, but it contained the essence. Folks would pay money for it. . . . That night a composer was born, an *American* composer. Those country blackboys had taught me something that could not possibly have been gained from books, something that would, however, cause books to be written."

From that moment on Handy began experimenting with this new kind of popular music, featuring it at his band concerts. As if by sudden magic, the popularity of the band grew, until it became known far and wide—eagerly invited and enthusiastically received. At the same time Handy began writing a new kind of music (he had been composing songs all this while) in which he hoped to capture something of the appeal of the melancholy, spiritual-like wail he had heard the Negro chant at the railroad station. At the same time he aspired to combine it with the appeal of popular music. The pieces he had composed up to this time were in the formal pattern of the popular song of the period. Now, for the first time, he was guided by the necessity of evolving a new style for himself—a style which, when perfected, would become his own, his identifying speech.

It is now well known how the first of Handy's blues was born. A mayoralty campaign was held in Memphis in 1909 in which one of the candidates, a man named Crump, was running on a reform ticket. Handy decided to write a campaign song called "Mr. Crump." Because he wanted to rally the votes of Beale Street to a platform as decidedly unpopular as that of reform, Handy decided to write a tune in his new idiom which he knew would appeal strongly to all the habitués of Memphis' street of pleasure. He thought of the strange melody he had heard at the lonely railroad station. Inspired by that recollection, he wrote a melody of his own.

The melody Handy wrote for his candidate refused to die, even long after the excitement of the election had ebbed. It remained alive in Memphis because Memphis had recognized it as a native expression. Its continued popularity inspired Handy to publish the song at his own expense. Under a new title, "Memphis Blues," it eventually achieved national fame. It was the first of the blues to be published.

"Memphis Blues" came to New York by way of a shrewd publisher who had bought all the rights of the song from Handy for fifty dollars. Originally refused by every established publisher before Handy had issued it himself, it now became a sensation. Single-handed it was destined to start a vogue for a new kind of popular music.

Disappointed that the great national success of his "Memphis Blues" had brought him no revenue, Handy turned to the writing of a successor from which he might profit more directly. He rented a room in Memphis' Beale Street—away from his family—and, in solitude, explored his imagination for a new "Memphis Blues."

To quote from his autobiography: "A flood of memories filled my mind. First there was the picture I had of myself, broke, unshaven, wanting even a decent meal, and standing before the lighted saloon in St. Louis without a shirt under my frayed coat. There was also from that same period a curious and dramatic little fragment that till now seemed to have little or no importance. While occupied with my own miseries during the sojourn, I had seen a woman whose pain seemed even greater. She had tried to take the edge off her grief by heavy drinking, but it hadn't worked. Stumbling along the poorly lighted street, she muttered as she walked, 'My man's got a heart like a rock cast in the sea.' . . . By the time I had finished all this heavy thinking and remembering, I figured it was time to get something down on paper, so I wrote 'I hate to see de evenin' sun go down.' If you ever had to sleep on the cobbles down by the river in St. Louis, you'll understand the complaint."

And so the "St. Louis Blues" was born. It was Handy's masterpiece, the high-water mark of his career. What happened thereafter—his triumphs and his tragedies—was anticlimactic. He was to write more than sixty other blues—among them such famous pieces as "Beale Street Blues," "Yellow Dog Blues," "John Henry Blues," "Aunt Hagar's Children," "Sundown Blues," "Friendless Blues," "Basement Blues," "Harlem Blues," "Joe Turner Blues," etc.

If Handy is today a hero to Memphis (a public park is named after him), if he is one of the great men in American popular music (he was listed at the New York World's Fair among the six hundred leading contributors to American culture) , and if on the occasion of his sixty-fifth birthday a stirring tribute was paid to him at Carnegie Hall, it was not because of his many melodies, some of which are poignant and effective, but because of the "St. Louis Blues."

It was not an immediate hit. Despite the fact that the "Memphis Blues" was known and helped to spread the blues nationally, the "St. Louis Blues" was refused by every important publisher. It was in order to publish his song that Handy finally organized a publishing house of his own in partnership with Harry Pace. Before long the company moved to New York and, now solidly entrenched with a hit which Sophie Tucker helped to make famous, it set out to sell the "St. Louis Blues" to America. The Victor Company was induced by Pace to make a recording of it. The record sold well, and every rival company issued it in one form or another. Player-piano rolls next were released. Then the sheet music began to move. It was a success. Bands throughout the country played it and found that audiences asked for it more and more insistently.

But the "St. Louis Blues" was destined for a more important fate than the popularity that attends an attractive novelty. It has become one of the classics of our popular musical literature; if any popular song survives our own day, surely it will be the "St. Louis Blues." It has been featured in special arrangements by every popular band and orchestra in existence, and it has helped to make stars of performers like Gilda Gray and Sophie Tucker. It has sold more records than any other single work in either the classical or the popular field. It has been used in a Broadway revue, in a movie short, in a full-length film. It has provided the title for three different movies and for a radio program. It is still reputed to earn about $25,000 a year from royalties.

Few will deny that it is one of the authentic native voices in our music. As such it has become a reigning favorite throughout the world. When Premier MacDonald of Great Britain visited America, a special orchestra conducted by Nathaniel Shilkret performed for him four distinctive American works, one of which was the "St. Louis Blues." King Edward VIII asked the pipers of Scotland to play it for him, and Queen Elizabeth of England has listed it as one of her favorite numbers. When Prince George of England and Princess Marina of Greece were married, the royal pair danced to its strains. When Ethiopia was invaded by Italy, Handy's classic became something of an Ethiopian battle hymn, frequently performed by the royal band in front of Haile Selassie's palace.

But much of this is only the tinsel with which to decorate and glamorize one salient fact: the "St. Louis Blues" is one of the undisputed masterpieces in our popular music. More than that, it has been a great influence. Without it jazz would hardly have developed in the form and style that it did. The "blues note," the "blues chord," the "break"—all became indispensable features of jazz. Beyond this, Handy's blues contributed technical features to hot music and to sweet music, to swing, to symphonic jazz, and to boogie-woogie. No other single work played such a decisive role in our popular musical development, and no other single work is more likely to remain one of the indestructible monuments in our popular musical expression.

♪♪

MEADE LUX LEWIS

On Chicago's South Side, the Negroes used to hold monthly parties to help raise money for the rent. At these parties, where the alcohol flowed and the human spirit was high, a noisy abandon prevailed. There would be dancing, and—of course—music. The music consisted of a piano on which Negro musicians would sometimes improvise melodies in keeping with the mood of these parties. It had to be a loud music to be heard above the din and confusion of the merrymakers. It had to be a music keyed with excitement and tension, sympathetic to the unleashed emotions of the audience. Because these parties were sometimes referred to as "pitchin' boogie," the name finally acquired by this piano music was "boogie-woogie."

It is believed that this name was first used in a composition by one of the pioneers of this style, Pine Top Smith. Pine Top Smith—so called because his conical head resembled a pine tree—was one of the true originators of boogie-woogie. Originally from St. Louis, he inspired those who heard him in Chicago to imitation —men like Yancey, for example. Besides writing the first real boogie-woogie blues, he made what are believed to be the first recordings of this piano jazz idiom. Pine Top was killed in a Chicago dance hall in 1928— a decade before boogie-woogie achieved nationwide fame.

One of the most favored of these early boogie pianists was Jim Yancey. During the early hours of dawn he would entertain his high-spirited audience with strangely cogent improvisations of the blues. After 1913, when he abandoned his career as vaudevillian, he devoted himself indefatigably to piano-playing, concentrating on blues melodies. He played all the time, for both his own and his friends' pleasure. To these performances he brought his own gift at improvisation, and succeeded in converting the blues into a piano expression of great and powerful surges.

Boogie-woogie thus emerged from the blues to become a piano idiom in its own right, an idiom marked by a relentless rhythmic drive. The left hand etched a brief rhythmic pattern (usually eight beats to the bar) which was repeated throughout the piece without variation; against this, the right hand created flights of melody. The effect was rhythmic rather than melodic. The resultant impression was not of a poignant blues melody, but a sweep of movement, a momentum, beginning with the first bar and rising in a crescendo of excitement to the last, leaving the hearers limp with spent emotions. It was a primitive expression—probably it harked back to its African origins—and it appealed to primitive instincts. It called for spontaneous emotional reactions of an almost kinesthetic sensation; it turned the head and quickened the pulse like strong alcohol.

2.

Boogie-woogie was the beloved form of musical entertainment on Chicago's South Side for more than a decade before it was discovered by the rest of the coun-

MEADE LUX LEWIS

try. In the middle 1930's the well-known critic and authority on hot jazz, John Henry Hammond, Jr., heard a boogie-woogie recording that made such a deep impression upon him that he decided to find its performer—a man named Meade Lux Lewis. But when he went to Chicago he was surprised to learn that no one seemed to know who or where Lewis was. This, however, merely spurred his search. He advertised in the newspapers. He hunted in every obscure night spot. Eventually his quest took him to the Club de Lisa, whose jazz band was led by a boogie-woogie artist named Albert Ammons. Ammons had known Lewis—indeed, they had had boogie-woogie sessions together —and was now prepared to help run him down. Together he and Hammond were eventually led to their man—washing cars in a garage.

It was then that Hammond learned something more about this remarkable jazz pianist. Born in Louisville, Kentucky, in 1905, the son of a Pullman porter, Lewis was taken to Chicago while still a child. He did not begin to study music (the violin) until his sixteenth year. One year later he heard Yancey play the piano blues, and at once became a convert to this type of music. He began to study the piano by himself, and then spent all his leisure time in playing blues and improvising them in the manner taught him by Yancey. He was living at the time in the same house with Pine Top Smith and Albert Ammons. Yancey would come here often, too, to play boogie-woogie with Smith. Thus, by descending a flight of stairs, both Ammons and Lewis were able to hear boogie-woogie at its best, and they were intoxicated by it. Ammons' house boasted a player-piano. Both Ammons and Lewis learned their first jazz pieces by setting the pianola into action and then, as the piano keys were depressed, following the depressions with their fingers.

For a living, Lewis took any job that presented itself, including that of driving a taxi for the Silver Taxicab Company. (Ammons, too, drove a cab for Silver.) But his hours of freedom belonged exclusively to boogie-woogie. He would play the piano at "pitchin' boogie" parties, for clubs, and in night spots. (When prohibition agents raided a club in which Lewis was performing, he would climb out of the window and hide under the ledge until the coast was clear.) His talent for improvisation was rich; he could frequently make elaborate melodic designs out of the simplest figures for a half-hour without lapsing into repetition. He even made records in 1927. It was one of these recordings—that of *Honky-Tonky Train*—that attracted Hammond.

The blues playing of Lewis and Ammons was the talk of the South Side. Frequently, Ammons and Lewis escaped from their assignments as taxi drivers to find a piano—and they were followed to their haunt by every other taxi-driver. It is said that the manager of the Silver Taxicab Company, unable at one time to find a single driver, decided to fit out a clubroom for his drivers (with a piano) so as to know where they were when he needed them.

It was Hammond's intention to bring Meade Lux Lewis—and with him, boogie-woogie—to the attention of the entire country. He arranged for Lewis to make some recordings, and helped him organize a little jazz band of his own. In May, 1936, Lewis was brought to New York to appear at a swing concert held at the

Imperial Theater. His performance did not make much of an impression, nor did his subsequent appearances at a basement restaurant in Greenwich Village. He returned to Chicago, convinced that neither he nor his music would ever be in popular demand. For a while he went on relief. But, on December 23, 1938, he was brought back to New York to appear with Ammons and Pete Johnson in an American Negro concert held at Carnegie Hall. They played in their best boogie-woogie manner—Johnson and Lewis on grand pianos, Ammons on an upright. And they took the audience by storm. As one writer remarked at the time: "The excitement mounted at such a pace that by the time the gentlemen had finished, it was necessary for the management to request the guests to come down from the chandeliers."

From that time on, the fame of Lewis—and boogie-woogie—was established. He was engaged for radio, for night clubs, and for recording sessions. With gems like *Bear Cat Crawl, Yancey Special, Honky-Tonky Train,* he established boogie-woogie as a major jazz style—the most important jazz style thus far to have been adapted for the piano.

♪

CHAPTER FIVE

DUKE ELLINGTON

"East Side, West Side . . . ."

DUKE ELLINGTON

♪

DUKE ELLINGTON

Ragtime bands had also arrived in New York. There were groups like the Five Ragtime Rubes (actually Brown's Band from Dixieland under a different name) and Will Johnson's New Orleans Band. Coming to New York by way of vaudeville, these bands found enthusiastic listeners. But it is now generally accepted that jazz made its official bow in New York on the evening of January 26, 1917. The event took place at a famous restaurant in Columbus Circle called Reisenweber's, which featured Nick La Rocca's Original Dixieland Jazz Band.

The band disgorged its voltaic music—a far cry from the formal waltzes, one-steps, tangos, and fox-trots to which New York had been accustomed. The music, with its piercing sonorities, its complicated rhythmic patterns, seemed like so much tonal confusion, so much riot of sound. Bewildered by this strange music, the clients at Reisenweber's made no move toward the dance floor, but listened—half perplexed, half magnetized. The band played one number after another—and still no move was made toward dancing. At last the manager interposed with a polite explanation: "Ladies and gentlemen, this is *jazz*. It is meant for dancing!" There was some good-humored laughter, and the ice was broken. A few venturesome partners started dancing; others followed. The music went to town, and so did the dancers. Jazz had come to New York. For better or for worse, it had come to stay.

Ragtime had had admirers in New York before 1912. But now, in 1917, it took the city by storm. The war in Europe had encouraged men in this country to work harder and live more intensely. In a few months America, too, would be knee-deep in the conflict—and the intensity of working and living would increase. The need of the times for some exciting diversion was answered by ragtime.

Still another factor was responsible for the instantaneous success of jazz. New York had, for several years now, been dance-crazy. In 1911 the Turkey Trot had helped to bring a certain degree of simplification to ballroom dancing, which had formerly required athleticism and youth. Dancing became so general a pastime—heightened in popularity through the magnetism of the incomparable Castles—that New York's leading hotels (recognizing the trend) introduced it officially with dining. By the time jazz arrived, everyone was dancing; and whoever danced was electrified by its rhythmic impulses and by the excitement it engendered. As *Variety* remarked in reporting the emergence of jazz at Reisenweber's: "There is one thing that is certain, and that is that the melodies as played by the jazz organization at Reisenweber's are quite conducive to making the dancers on the floor loosen up and go to the limit in their stepping." Besides, ragtime—with its even 2/4 and 4/4 beat—reduced simplicity to even further simplicity of movement, to a point where anyone who could move his feet rhythmically across a dance floor was capable of performing creditably.

2.

As long as Chicago was the capital of "real jazz," New York was only a suburban musical town. But, in spite of its comparative provincialism where jazz was concerned, good jazz could be heard there, and was admired. The numerous counterfeits of real jazz bands need not concern us. After the success of Nick La Rocca's band, innumerable little groups arose to imitate its style without even half guessing that there was more to ragtime than volume of sound and rapidity of tempo. But there was the Original Dixieland, which remained in New York until 1919. There was a second genuine New Orleans ensemble—the Louisiana Five. There was also the Original Memphis Five, a good northern approximation of the southern product. And, most important of them all, there was Fletcher Henderson's band—the first of New York's great Negro jazz ensembles.

The son of a schoolteacher, Henderson first studied chemistry, then turned to music by playing the piano in road shows. In 1919 he organized a jazz orchestra for Roseland in New York, where he remained (on and off) for fifteen years. Before long jazz devotees in New York were found in Roseland, sitting on the sidelines, listening to Fletcher's music. An excellent pianist and a brilliant arranger, Fletcher Henderson was a jazz musician of aristocratic breed. To his orchestra (the first, incidentally, to feature full brass, reed, and rhythm sections) he brought the best available instrumentalists and encouraged brilliant solo playing. Under his direction, the playing of the orchestra had beautiful fluidity of tonal movement, producing a feeling of utter relaxation and spontaneity without sacrificing the rhythmic momentum and full-textured sonorities. It was not a hot band in today's sense. Improvisation was subordinated to Fletcher's elegant but simply conceived orchestrations, with their effective writing for sections, their rich harmonic colorings, their wonderful sense for climaxes. The men had to read the music and submerge their own instincts and urges. It will be recalled that when Louis Armstrong joined this orchestra he felt constricted by its discipline. But it was excellent jazz in its own right, exploiting the best qualities of best jazz. And it pointed to the full potentialities of the large jazz orchestra.

Before Fletcher Henderson withdrew as conductor to devote himself primarily to orchestration, another great jazz orchestra appeared in New York. It held a position of incomparable importance—a position which it still holds to this very day. It was one of several major factors in transferring the capital of jazz from Chicago to New York. This orchestra was the creation of one of jazz's major personalities, perhaps one of the major musical personalities of our time.

The name, of course, is Duke Ellington.

3.

Early in 1943 the Duke celebrated the twentieth anniversary of his career as bandleader. No one grudged him his celebration, or denied that he had good cause for rubbing his hands with satisfaction. He found himself Number One Man in Jazz—officially so, according to the 1942 poll of *Down Beat* among some

15,000 musicians. At a Carnegie Hall concert on January 23 (his first in that holy hall) he introduced a new three-movement work, a "tonal parallel to the history of the Negro in America," called *Black, Brown and Beige,* which brought him the accolade of the intelligentsia. But actually these fresh honors duplicated others gathered over many years. Musicians like Stokowski, Percy Grainger, and the well-known English composer and critic, Constant Lambert have sung his praises. Lambert went so far as to say that the Duke was "the most original musical mind in America," while Grainger found in the Duke's music qualities belonging to Bach, Mozart, and Delius. Ellington has also been one of the first to give a concert of real jazz music at an institution of higher learning—Colgate University. And at New York University he gave an exhibition of his style and idiom at a serious music-appreciation course.

The "hot-lick" fans had, of course, long ago crowned him their king of kings. A one-man trust of jazz, who writes his own music, orchestrates it, then performs it, the Duke has been, these many years, in a class by himself. From time to time there have been bands more popular than his; but none has held the admiration and affection of its admirers so sustainedly and uninterruptedly. Often he has been imitated, but never successfully. "Hell," remarked one famous jazz musician, "to imitate the Duke, well you've got to be the Duke, or else you're wasting your time."

A big, genial fellow with an even temper and a deeply religious nature (his favorite book is the Bible), he appears off the bandstand mild-mannered to a point of gentleness. Yet put him at the piano in front of his men and he suddenly becomes charged with volts. That man's got rhythm, and plenty besides. He quivers with music as though he were wired for sound. His inner magnetism creates sparks which set aflame the men who play under him. He becomes a victim of inner compulsions.

It was that way even many years ago. In one of the first orchestra jobs he ever held he was suddenly and uncontrollably led to insert a "break" that was not in the score. He gave all that was in him. A moment later he was without a job.

Since that time he has formulated the musical philosophy which has, first instinctively, then more consciously, guided him—"It don't mean a thing if it ain't got swing." He is always there swinging—and producing a music that is for him as natural an expression as breathing. Actually he does not like to refer to his music as jazz or swing. He considers it Negro music, expressive of his race, and evolved from centuries of Negro music-making. But it is still jazz and swing of the highest order. His music has irresistible rhythmic drive, with brilliant splashes of instrumental color, with stunning effects and sonorities and sound combinations.

His music takes your breath away. The staid critic of the London *Times* once remarked somewhat professorially about Ellington that "the excitement and exacerbation of the nerves which are caused by the performances of his orchestra are the more disquieting by reason of his complete control and precision. It is not an orgy, but a scientific application of measured and dangerous stimuli." What he meant was that the Duke quickens your pulse and heartbeat and does it through subtle musical forces rather than through a wild orgy of rhythms and shrieking sounds. His music has an inner excitement. It has nerves. It has intensity. The rhythm is there, but it is made secondary to rich harmonic and contrapuntal devices and to many-colored orchestrations.

As the jazz musician had remarked, "To imitate the Duke, well you've got to be the Duke." Many have tried to reduce the Ellington formula into its component elements—with the hope, no doubt, of discovering the secret of the man's musical magnetism. He has always had a wonderful band of musicians (most of them, like the trumpeter "Cootie" Williams, trombonist Joe "Tricky" Nanton, and saxophonist Johnny Hodges, virtuosos of the first order). They understand him to a point where his lifted eyebrow or quivering nostril conveys to them a definite musical message. They have developed ensemble playing of such integration and relaxation that it has become an art in itself.

Then there are Ellington's distinctive orchestrations, rich textures of musical sound, extraordinarily varied in shading, color, nuances. Particularly eloquent are his combinations of horns. Make no mistake about it—the Duke combines science and instinct to a highly sensitized point where arranging, too, becomes a fine art. Finally, there is Ellington's original music—a long parade of musical successes like "Solitude" (which won the ASCAP $2,500 prize). "Mood Indigo," "Bojangles," "Portrait of Bert Williams," and "Sophisticated Lady," which have become jazz classics. This original music uses jazz writing with striking effect. Add all these elements together—performance, orchestration, and original creation—and you have Ellington's art, one of the most successful realizations of a real jazz style up to the present time.

Yet this analysis does not altogether explain the Duke's inimitable style and manner. Others have good bands; others exploit wonderfully effective orchestrations; others have written fine jazz pieces. It is certainly possible to combine all these three harmoniously—even if they are not all three the products of one man. But no matter how you combine them, the result is never Ellington. It may be good jazz, but it isn't the Duke's jazz, which remains a thing radically apart from the jazz of any other living musician.

Perhaps the secret becomes more easily discoverable at an Ellington rehearsal. It usually begins after the evening's work is over—about three in the morning—and keeps up until about dawn. At these rehearsals Ellington completes his orchestrations. His men help him along—giving him suggestions for a unique instrumental effect here, a striking solo passage there. Ellington tries out all ideas, working them into a coherent pattern. An Ellington orchestration is the result of experimentation, painstaking rehearsal, trial and error. In playing the music of others, he uses little more than the original melodic subject. The instrumentation, the developments, the "breaks," the embellishments, are all his own.

The Duke composes his own music in much the same way he prepares his orchestrations. He comes to his rehearsals with the germ of an idea, plays it to the boys, and listens to their suggestions on what should be done with it. The germs themselves come to him easily. "Sophisticated Lady" was sketched out on the back of a dirty envelope in a taxi, on his way to a per-formance. "Solitude" came to him in a few minutes before one of his radio programs. But working them into an elaborate pattern of an effective piece of music takes a great deal of hard work—and in this his men help him no end.

There is this wonderful give-and-take between the Duke and his men which is probably at least half the explanation of the Duke's unique powers. They have worked together a long time, know each other's idio-syncrasies, sympathize with one another and, most im-portant of all, respect and admire each other. On the bandstand the Duke treats his men like partners, though no one denies his authority or the fact that he is the integrating force. Off the bandstand, he acts like the father of a brood of children, solicitous about his men's troubles, their problems and daily conflicts. They learned long ago to confide in him when some-thing bothers them, and they find him both concerned over their troubles and generous when the need arises. It is this wonderful partnership, in music and out of it, that makes possible the co-ordination of effort and temperament which is one of the identifying trade-marks of all Ellington's performances.

His music brings him a large income and permits him (on stage and off) to indulge in a touch of flam-boyance in both dress and manner which is an expres-sion of his temperament. Even as a boy, he liked to dress snappily and live in style. His friends, in those days, gave him the sobriquet which has since stuck to him—"the Duke." The son of a blueprint tracer for the Navy Yard, the Duke was born as Edward Ken-nedy Ellington in Washington, D. C., in April, 1899.

He first began studying the piano at the age of seven, and later on, finding practicing dull, would spend all his time improvising tunes.

He planned to become an artist, spurred on in this ambition by a scholarship at Pratt Institute, which he won in his last year at high school. A temporary job as a soda-jerker in a combination ice-cream parlor and poolroom changed his destiny. A piano there attracted the Duke in his off moments to give vent to the music within him, much to the delight of the clients. One of these, impressed by what he heard, gave the Duke an opportunity to play in a band. That one performance convinced the Duke that there was only one future for him—the making of music.

He was seventeen when, asked to play in a society band, he was given his first indication of his possible future as a jazz stylist. On the spur of the moment—in playing his music he was always to be a victim of momentary whims and impulses—he decided to imitate the dashing piano style of Lucky Robert, who would lift his hands dramatically from the keyboard on finishing an electrifying passage. "Before I knew it the kids around the stand were screaming with delight and clapped for more. In two minutes the flashy hands had earned me a reputation, and after that I was all set."

It was not long before he formed a band of his own and filled various small assignments in Washington. When he was twenty-four, he came to New York, worked in several theaters with Wilbur Sweatman's jazz band, performed at rent parties in Harlem, and then formed a five-piece band of his own for the Kentucky Club.

The zest of his playing, combined with his novel and intriguing orchestrations, attracted quite a bit of attention. Lovers of hot jazz came regularly to the Kentucky Club expressly to hear the Duke's magnetizing performances. An exponent of a true jazz style, with his off-beat rhythms, blues harmonies, free improvisations, and intriguing contrapuntal effects, he found a cohort of disciples ready to worship him. One of these was the publisher Irving Mills, who immediately placed Ellington's name on a contract. Mills helped Ellington increase his band to twelve players, got him a recording date, and then landed him a choice booking at the Cotton Club in Harlem (later moved to downtown Broadway).

"We came in with a new style," the Duke explained to an interviewer.* "Our playing was stark and wild and tense. That's the way our boys had to play, and we planned our music that way. We tried new effects. One of our trombones turned up one night with an ordinary kitchen pot for his sliphorn. It sounded good. We let him keep it, until we could get him a handsomer gadget that gave him the same effects. We put the Negro feeling and spirit in our music. We were not the first to do that, but maybe we added some more. We did it in a different way. Other bands came along later and did similar things, though not quite the same."

From this time on things developed rapidly for the Duke. He made about fifteen hundred master recordings, and his records sold fabulously, especially in England. In 1940 the magazine *Swing* selected seven-

---

* Howard Taubman, "The Duke Invades Carnegie Hall," *The New York Times* Magazine, January 17, 1943.

teen Ellington recordings among the twenty-eight best of the year. He scored over the air on all the networks, starred in a Ziegfeld show (*Show Girl,* the music of which was written by George Gershwin), made personal appearances in practically every major theater in the country, and subsequently was featured in several talking pictures. Feeling that this country had become too small for his conquests, the Duke made two trips to Europe. In 1933 he was toasted and feted in London and Paris. In 1939 he gave twenty-eight concerts on as many consecutive nights in France, Holland, Norway, Denmark, and Sweden, sending the European capitals—over which hovered the dark shadow of impending war—into a jazz orgy that momentarily lightened their fears.

CHAPTER SIX

PAUL WHITEMAN
FERDE GROFÉ

"Soft Lights And Sweet Music . . . ."

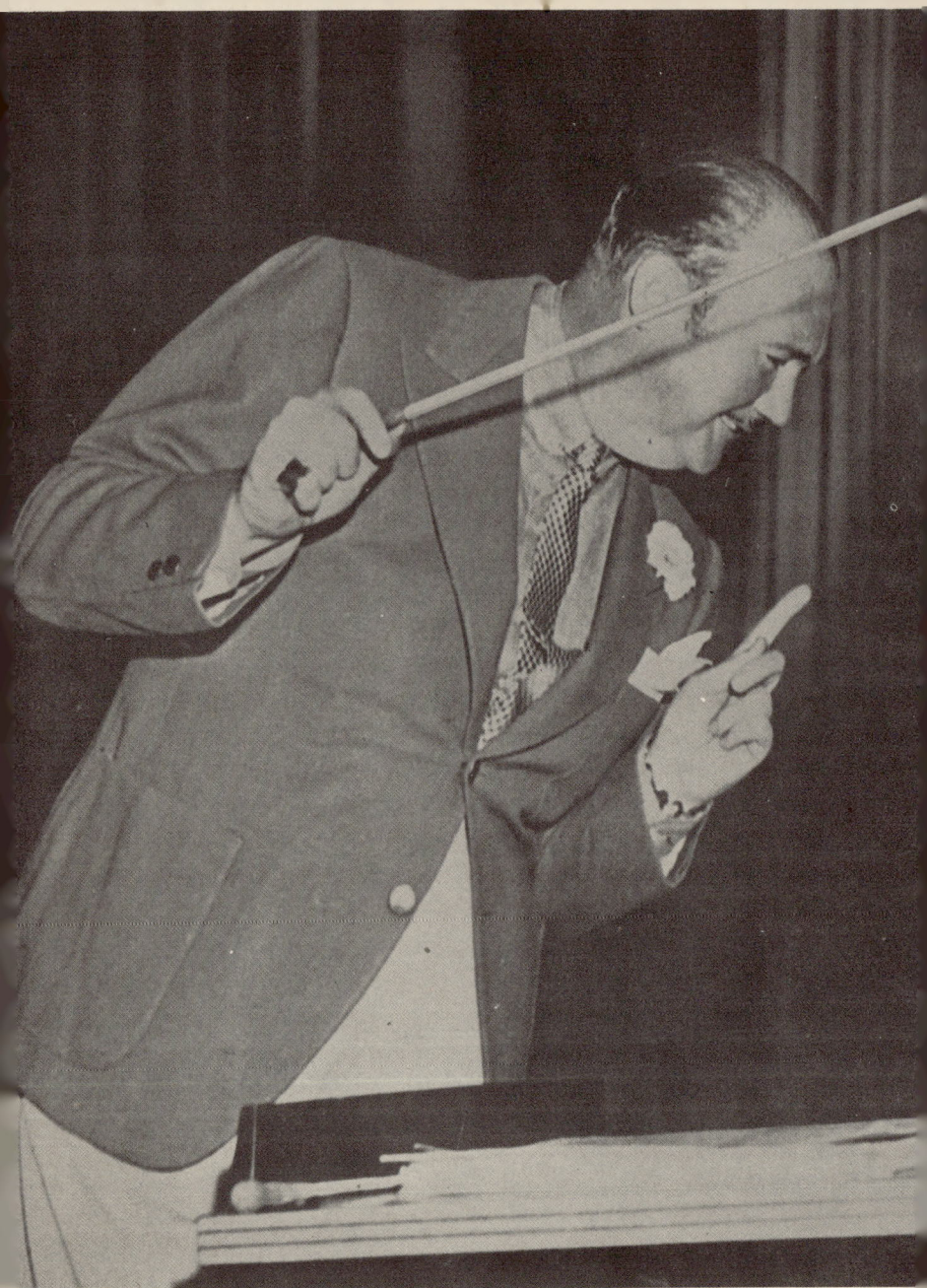

PAUL WHITEMAN

♪

PAUL WHITEMAN
FERDE GROFÉ

The jazz which the entire country was soon to learn and to accept as its favored form of popular music was not the jazz which had been born in New Orleans, apotheosized in Chicago, and transplanted to New York. It was, rather, a hybrid product, combining some of the rhythmic elements of ragtime, some of the melodic and harmonic devices of the blues, and adding to these some elements of its own, principally in the field of symphonic orchestration. Its high priest was Paul Whiteman. "All I did," wrote Paul Whiteman somewhat modestly in his autobiography, "was to orchestrate jazz. If I had not done it, somebody else would have. The time was ripe for that. Conditions produce the men, not men the conditions. It merely happened that I was the fortunate person who combined the idea, the place, the time."

But Whiteman is minimizing his contribution. He not only was the agent for bringing good orchestration to popular music, but more than any other single person he was responsible for crystallizing jazz style and giving it the form and substance it was henceforth to retain. Through his performances—and through his encouragement to American composers—he opened up altogether new vistas for American popular music. He recognized that the jazz playing of his time had an elemental power; but he also felt that this power had to be harnessed. What ragtime needed, he knew, was artistic discipline—that and the enrichment that the resources of symphonic writing could bring to it. The spontaneous improvisation of ragtime players had a fascination all its own. To that fascination Whiteman, too, had succumbed. But music built exclusively on improvisation represented an extreme. What was needed now was some calculation, some artistic planning, some preconceived design and construction by men who were masters of their trade. Whiteman, accordingly, introduced skillful orchestrations, symphonic in their use of harmony, counterpoint, and thematic development; this was the work of expert arrangers whose skill with musical technique was adroit. Whiteman had his jazz musicians follow the printed page during performances which were meticulously rehearsed. Beyond this, Whiteman subdued the intensity of jazz expression. He believed in "sweet" music as opposed to "hot": more strings, less brass; more harmony and melody, less rhythm; a greater contrast in dynamics—more *piano,* less *fortissimo.*

His pioneer work was completed many years ago. That he is still a major figure in jazz—important enough to receive in 1943 an appointment as musical director of the Blue Network—is a tribute to his musicianship and his capacity to grow and develop. But, even if his popularity has not greatly waned, his influential days are over. He is best known today—and he will be best remembered tomorrow—not because he was the conductor of an excellent orchestra, and the sympathetic interpreter of good jazz, but because he was a pioneer of epochal importance. Without him it would have been impossible for our popular music to reach the stage of development it has at present.

Devotees of hot jazz sometimes tend to depreciate his importance; they go even farther and insist that he only adulterated what had originally been the *true* jazz style. Yet one of the greatest of all hot-jazz performers has conceded Whiteman's significance. "Don't let them kid you about Whiteman," Duke Ellington told an interviewer. "He has been a big man in our music. He has done a lot for it, especially with his concerts where he gave composers a chance to write new, extended works." Whiteman did this, and more too. In brief, he was one of the first of our important popular musicians to attempt to bridge the then unbridged gap between serious and popular music. When that fusion was completed, our popular music was well on its way toward artistic significance, and toward recognition by the entire world as a vital American expression.

2.

It was perhaps inevitable that Whiteman should have thought along the lines of merging into one the two worlds of popular and serious music. For he had come to jazz by way of serious music. Born on March 28, 1890, in Denver, Colorado, he was the son of excellent musicians. His father was Wilberforce J. Whiteman, director of music education in the Denver public schools. His mother was a singer in oratorio. Paul grew up in an atmosphere saturated with good music. It cannot be said, however, that he responded to these strong musical influences at first. Taught the violin at an early age, he refused to practice, and at one time defiantly told his father that he did not like music and would have nothing further to do with it. When his father scolded him severely, Paul, in an uncontrolled fit of temper, smashed his violin over the flywheel of a sewing machine.

His conversion to good music was so sudden that he himself is at a loss to identify its immediate cause. All he remembers today is that he suddenly began to react to good music with a strange intensity of affection. The singing of Schubert songs by his mother could provoke a fever in him. While attending concerts by artists such as Kreisler, Ysaye, and Paderewski, or performances of opera, he would sit through the music as if in a trance, oblivious to everyone and everything except the music.

He now studied the violin enthusiastically with his father and later with Max Bendix, acquiring a sufficient command of the instrument to be appointed to the Denver Symphony Orchestra. By 1907 he rose to the position of first violinist. This, however, was only one part of his intimate association with good music. Subsequently, he played in the San Francisco People's Symphony Orchestra, and was a member of a string quartet.

But, almost from the beginning of his professional career, he aspired to make a name for himself in popular music. When he was a member of the Denver Symphony, he would gather a few musicians and lead them in "rag" performances of the classics. In San Francisco he became acquainted with good ragtime for the first time. A friend of his—in an effort to cure him of a sudden spell of the blues—took him to a dive on the Barbary Coast which specialized in hot music.

The experience proved unforgettable. "My whole body," Whiteman says, "began to sit up and take notice. It was like coming out of the blackness into the bright light. My blues faded when treated to the Georgia blues that some trombonist was wailing about. My head was dizzy, and my feet seemed to understand that tune. They began to pat wildly. I wanted to whoop. I wanted to dance. I wanted to sing. I did them all. Raucous? Yes. Crude? Undoubtedly. Unmusical? Sure as you live. But rhythmic, catching as the smallpox and spirit-lifting. That was jazz then. I liked it, though it puzzled me. Even then it seemed to me to have vitality, sincerity, and truth in it. In spite of its uncouthness, it was trying to say something peculiarly American, just as an uneducated man struggles ungrammatically to express a true and original idea. . . . The fantastic beat drummed in my ears long after the strident echoes had died, and sleep for nights became a saxophonic mockery."*

It was not long before Whiteman decided that his place was with popular and not serious music. Perhaps he was already fired with the ideal of bringing a good syntax and grammar to the undisciplined and ill-bred speech of the music he had heard in the dive. At any rate, he abandoned his orchestra post and found a spot in a jazz band. After two days he was dismissed because he could not integrate his own style of violin-playing with that of ragtime. For the next few months he devoted himself seriously to an extensive study of jazz style. He went from one restaurant to another, listening to any and every jazz band, and

* Paul Whiteman and Mary Margaret McBride, "Jazz" (New York: J. H. Sears & Co., 1926).

trying to dissect the idiom. In his room he experimented endlessly on his violin, improvising jazz rhythms, intonations, breaks.

Then, when he felt that he had assimilated the new language, he set out to speak it with a band of his own. Gathering a few high-spirited and ambitious youngsters, he formed an ensemble and put it through the paces of rigorous rehearsing. The band never made a public appearance. At one of the rehearsals the news came that America had entered the war. The band was instantly disrupted. Its leader joined the Navy. And it was in the Navy that Whiteman got his first major experience in leading a group of musicians in a post as bandleader.

After the war Whiteman led an orchestra at the Fairmont Hotel in San Francisco. Ill health forced him to abandon this assignment. When he recovered, he filled one job after another directing orchestras in California. He saved his money parsimoniously, for he was now guided by one and only one ambition: to found and direct an orchestra of his own.

A California hotel man named John Hernan interested himself in Whiteman and made it possible for him to realize his ambition through an engagement at the Alexandria Hotel in Los Angeles. Whiteman's debut was attended by many leading motion-picture stars, who were delighted with his suave performance. Their stamp of approval on him, Whiteman's success was reasonably assured. He remained at the Alexandria Hotel for one year, and—as proof of his success—the cover receipts rose in that time from three hundred dollars a day to twelve hundred.

The permanency of his orchestra was now assured.

Whiteman began to experiment more and more with the quality and texture of his performances. He knew what he wanted: a blend of symphonic technique with the spirit and style of jazz. His experiences in symphony orchestras had taught him that jazz could profit immeasurably through the assimilation of the developed rhythmic, harmonic, and contrapuntal vocabulary of great music.

A good orchestra, carefully trained, was only a partial answer to Whiteman's search. He knew well that the acquisition of a first-class arranger—a man who had musical technique at his fingertips and could combine skill and taste and imagination—was equally important. Such an arranger could fashion a symphonic mold for jazz.

In 1919 Whiteman stepped into a dance hall and there was struck by the music he heard. What attracted him particularly was the subtlety of the orchestration, its delicate tints and hues, its luscious texture, its beautifully blended sonorities. Whiteman approached the stout, round-faced orchestra leader and inquired who the band's arranger was. "Why," the leader answered, "I do all the arrangements myself."

Then and there Whiteman engaged the orchestra leader as the pianist and arranger for his own orchestra. Thus began the collaboration of Paul Whiteman and Ferde Grofé—and with it Whiteman's international fame.

3.

Ferde Grofé's career closely parallels that of Paul Whiteman. He, too, was the son of an excellent musician. His mother had graduated from the Leipzig Conservatory and was a gifted 'cellist (she later became the teacher of the present-day conductor, Alfred Wallenstein). Like Whiteman, furthermore, Grofé came to jazz along the highway of good music. Born in New York City on March 27, 1892 (his name originally was Ferdinand Rudolph von Grofé), he began to study music at the age of five, and at nine began composing pieces for chamber-music groups.

While he was still a boy, his father died, and his mother remarried. His new father wanted him to become either a banker or a lawyer, and was none too favorable to Ferdinand's musical inclinations. At the age of fourteen, therefore, Ferde ran away from home. "There was too much stepfather and too many stepsisters and stepbrothers at home," he later explained to an interviewer. Actually he was running away from any future unrelated to music. For the next few years he supported himself as best he could, earning his living as a pressman in a bookbindery, driving a truck, ushering in a theater, operating an elevator, working in an iron foundry, and selling milk. It was not long before, after a circuitous route, he came back to music. He joined up with a wandering cornet-player named "Professor" Albert Jerome. "We were in a mining town called Winthrop in a gulch in Northern California when he ran out on me, taking all the money and leaving me with an unpaid board bill. The only job I could get was playing the piano in a sporting house—that's what they were called then—for two dollars a night. I didn't get corrupted because I was in love with my landlady's daughter."

Grofé's family, shocked to learn that he was working

in a den of vice, decided to yield to his musical ambitions. Ferde returned home in 1909, and soon afterward joined the Los Angeles Symphony Orchestra as violist (his grandfather had once been first 'cellist of that orchestra, and his uncle a concertmaster). For ten years Grofé remained with that orchestra, acquiring in that time a comprehensive knowledge of symphonic literature. To this day his tastes in music reflect his background: his favorite composers are Ravel and Sibelius.

He combined work in a symphony orchestra with random engagements in jazz bands. He was a banjoist in the first ragtime band to hit San Francisco, later a pianist in another. Ragtime fascinated him. Because he did not wish to forget the wonderful effects that were produced in spontaneous ragtime performances, he began putting them down on paper. It was not long before he had a band of his own. With it he introduced written novel arrangements of popular tunes, arrangements richly symphonic in treatment. It was while he was leading one of these bands that Whiteman discovered him and engaged him for his own orchestra.

Every single number featured by Whiteman was orchestrated by Grofé. He proved himself to be an ace arranger. One of the first orchestrations he made for Whiteman, "Whispering," sold more than a million and a half records. He was to become the first of that brilliant group of orchestrators which would include men like Robert Russell Bennett and Morton Gould; and up to the present time he has remained one of the best. Of his mastery of instrumentation there has never been a question; as a matter of fact, he subsequently joined the faculty of the Juilliard School of Music in the department of orchestration. Not only does he have a consummate command of all the instruments of the orchestra, but he also knows how to combine them into fascinating sonorities, and how to produce piquant tone qualities. To popular music he has brought a wealth of harmonic and rhythmic resources which he assimilated during his years in symphonic music; and he has combined this with imagination, inventiveness in conceiving new colors and effects. He has also shown daring and independence in his use of unusual timbres and effects—the same daring that later enabled him to use with such effectiveness a typewriter ·(in *Tabloid*), sirens and pneumatic drills (in *Symphony in Steel*), a bicycle pump (in *Free Air*), and the banging of carpenters and the barking of directors (in *Hollywood Suite*).

In his own compositions Grofé was later to reveal himself a master of the tools of composition. But even in his earliest arrangements for Whiteman, it became obvious that here was a technician of the first order. Whiteman's music had aristocratic distinction, which the music of no other jazz ensemble at the time could imitate. At least half the secret rested in Grofé's musically conceived arrangements. He had ability to take a jaded or stereotyped tune and dress it in new harmonic colors until it became bright and sparkling. When he had in his hands a really original melody—a song by Berlin, Gershwin, or Kern, or a remarkable larger work like *Rhapsody in Blue*—his wizardry could evoke from the music new subtleties of expression and nuances which amazed even their composers. Even in his jazz arrangements of the classics—in my

FERDE GROFÉ

opinion, the least creditable of his products—there could be no doubt that, for better or for worse, the transplantation had been achieved with astuteness.

In 1924 Grofé left Whiteman to become a free-lance arranger. He was to continue to be the prince of the kingdom, and to this distinction he was soon to add that of being a composer of excellent serious music in the jazz style. His best original works include the *Mississippi Suite, Metropolis* (which contains the first fugue ever to be written in the jazz idiom), *Three Shades of Blue, Tabloid, Hollywood, Symphony in Steel, Café Society,* and one of the accepted classics in the jazz repertoire, the *Grand Canyon Suite.* Grofé was also to make his mark as a conductor of orchestras, making his official debut at Carnegie Hall early in 1937. Yet, as we evaluate his career, we are tempted to say—even in the face of our admiration of his creative gifts—that he has proved most important in his role as Whiteman's arranger. For out of his collaboration with Whiteman developed a jazz language which has been heard around the world and which has influenced the direction of our popular music.

Jazz was emancipated on the afternoon of Lincoln's Birthday in 1924. It was then that Paul Whiteman conducted a program of "American music" at Aeolian Hall in New York.

It was not the first time that jazz had entered the concert auditorium. As early as 1914 the Negro jazz band leader, Jim Europe, had directed a concert of ragtime in Carnegie Hall. A more significant effort to bring jazz into the realm of good music took place when on November 1, 1923, the singer Eva Gauthier included in her song recital (together with works by Purcell, Byrd, Bellini, Bartók, Schönberg, Hindemith, and Milhaud) a group devoted exclusively to popular songs by Berlin, Kern, and Gershwin. In this "jazz" group her accompanist was Gershwin himself. "I consider this one of the very most important events in musical history," the novelist Carl Van Vechten wrote at the time. "I suggest we get up a torchlight procession headed by Paul Whiteman to honor Miss Gauthier, the pioneer."

Some three months after this came the Whiteman concert, also at Aeolian Hall—the first to feature an extended work written in the jazz idiom for large symphonic orchestra. Like Carnegie Hall, Aeolian had traditionally been sacrosanct to fine music; nobody had ever before dreamed of playing unorthodox programs there. Thus, when Whiteman planned to use it for jazz, he was flouting convention and inviting criticism.

In vain his friends tried to dissuade him. They argued that he would only bring ridicule on himself; that he had now reached the top of his profession and was earning a large income; that this position might be imperiled if now he sought to credit jazz with a musical importance it did not possess.

And Whiteman had truly traveled far since he had brought Grofé to his orchestra. An engagement at the Ambassador Hotel in Atlantic City had attracted the attention of the East. Numerous flattering offers came his way: a two-year contract with Victor records; a contract to play in vaudeville; an extended engagement at New York's swank night club, the Palais Royale. The press now referred to him as the "King of Jazz," and he was written up in articles and interviews. An engagement at the *Ziegfeld Follies* added to his success and made him a notable personality in the theater world. In the spring of 1923 he took his orchestra to Europe where it was enthusiastically received in the leading capitals.

All these triumphs might, his friends feared, count for nothing if now he attempted to import jazz into a dignified concert auditorium. Why, they begged, should the "King of Jazz" risk becoming the "clown of Aeolian Hall"?

But Whiteman remained deaf to dissuasion. Through music he had acquired everything he had set store on—everything except the realization of his lifelong ambition to make of jazz an important and respected musical language. In only one way could the music world's attention be drawn to the artistic possibilities of the jazz form: bring jazz directly into the world of serious music whatever the risk to himself.

Whiteman's program for the evening of February 12, 1924, frankly combined good and bad, in an attempt to portray all the varying facets of popular music. The first group contrasted the jazz of 1914 with that of 1924: the *Livery Stable Blues* was juxtaposed with "Mama Loves Papa." A second group highlighted comedy numbers like "Yes, We Have No Bananas." A third group emphasized the then new art of jazz orchestration as developed by Grofé. Still another group featured new jazz pieces by men like Jerome Kern and Zez Confrey. There were symphonic arrangements of popular melodies, and jazz arrangements of symphonic melodies. And, as the tenth number of the program—and the one that transformed Whiteman's concert from a novelty into a historic event—came the world première of a work written especially for that concert, and commissioned by Whiteman to give final proof to his theory that jazz could speak with dignity and self-respect in a form of major proportions: George Gershwin's *Rhapsody in Blue*.

The great of the music world flocked to the concert. The audience included Rachmaninoff, Godowsky, Sousa, Kreisler, Elman, Heifetz, Damrosch, Stokowski, Mengelberg, Stravinsky—and many others. Some had come out of healthy curiosity; others only to sneer. They all remained—particularly after listening to Gershwin's *Rhapsody*—to give homage to a pioneer who had enough prophetic faith in jazz to exhibit it to the world as a serious musical expression.

"Fifteen minutes before the concert was to begin," wrote Whiteman in his autobiography, "I yielded to a nervous longing to see for myself what was happening out front, and putting on an overcoat over my concert clothes, I slipped around to the entrance of Aeolian Hall.

"There I gazed upon a picture that should have imparted new vigor to my wilting confidence. It was snowing, but men and women were fighting to get into the door, pulling and mauling each other as they sometimes do at a baseball game, or a prize fight, or in the subway. Such was my state of mind at the time that I wondered if I had come to the right entrance. And then I saw Victor Herbert going in. It was the right entrance, sure enough, and the next day the ticket-office people said they could have sold out the house ten times over.

"I went back stage again, more scared than ever.

Black fear simply possessed me. I paced the floor, gnawed my thumbs, and vowed I'd give five thousand dollars if I could stop right then and there. Now that the audience had come, perhaps I had really nothing to offer them at all. I even made excuses to keep the curtain from rising on schedule. But finally there was no longer any way of postponing the evil moment. The curtain went up and before I could dash forth, as I was tempted to do, and announce that there wouldn't be any concert, we were in the midst of it."

4.

Whiteman had gambled, and—though the odds had been against him—he had won. That concert entrenched him permanently as the monarch of jazz. For the next decade he was to the nation a synonym for jazz music at its best. He appeared in Broadway theaters, at night clubs, on the vaudeville stage, in concert halls, on the screen, and over the air—duplicating one great success with another. That concert—no doubt about it!—had been the greatest personal triumph of his career.

But perhaps the richest satisfaction he derived from this concert was the assurance that it was an even greater triumph for jazz. Henceforth jazz was to receive the attention it deserved as an artistic force and as a native American expression. Although before 1924 a few venturesome composers—Stravinsky in *Piano Ragtime*, Milhaud in *La Création du Monde*, and Erik Satie in *Parade*—had dabbled with jazz idiom, it was rather in the spirit of a respectable businessman going slumming—for an exciting contact with a forbidden pleasure. Only after 1924 did jazz have an obvious serious purpose in music. Thenceforth it was to be a major idiom, treated with artistic sincerity. Serious composers like Ravel, Křenek, Hindemith, Copland, Milhaud, Lambert, William Walton, Louis Gruenberg—they, and many others as well, were to use jazz as the basis of serious composition.

Beyond this, jazz had now become a national disease. With its ragtime abandon and intoxication sobered by a touch of sentimentality, it was the favored speech of a feverish era—the fabulous twenties. It was the decade of the hipflask, the speakeasy, the flapper; of Dorothy Parker cynicism and Clara Bow sex appeal. Skirts were high and morals low. The pursuit of pleasure was glorified as the greatest good; law-breaking took on the status of a schoolboyish prank. Sensationalism was fed and encouraged on the screen, in the theater, and by the tabloid which was an offspring of this period. Faddism was rampant. The era was emotionally high-pitched, full of tensions, touched even by suggestions of hysteria. Racy literature echoed the spirit of the times. And so did jazz. The moan of the saxophone (as one writer aptly wrote) was like the wail of a lost generation. The nervous accent of syncopation was like the quickening heartbeat of the younger generation geared to fast living.

Because jazz was confused with the evils and emancipations of the era it interpreted, there were those reformers who denounced it vitriolically. Jazz, they insisted, promoted immorality, alcoholism, and even insanity. One educator found that "its influence is as harmful and degrading to civilized races as it always has been among the savages from whom we borrowed it. If we permit our boys and girls to be exposed indefinitely to this pernicious influence, the harm that will result may tear to pieces our whole social fabric." A physician tried to prove scientifically that jazz caused inebriation without benefit of alcohol. Jazz, he argued, sends "a continuous whirl of impressionable stimulations to the brain, producing thoughts and imaginations which overpower the will. Reason and reflection are lost, and the actions of the person are directed by the stronger animal passions. In other words, jazz affects the brain through the sense of hearing, giving the same results as whisky or any other alcoholic drinks taken into the system by way of the stomach. It has the same effect as a drug, and one may become addicted to its use." The president of the Christian and Missionary Alliance Conference charged that "American girls of tender age are approaching jungle standards. . . . Little American girls are maturing too quickly under the hectic influence of jazz."

But jazz found its articulate defenders as well. Its sponsors realized its sound values would persist long after the fever of the twenties had subsided, and health and normalcy returned. Such American musicians as Leopold Stokowski, Fritz Kreisler, and John Alden Carpenter spoke for its musical importance. Daniel Gregory Mason, never one of jazz's advocates, confessed that it had "a kind of democratic inclusiveness and Whitmanesque cordiality." Maurice Ravel told one American composer that an American music of importance could be evolved only through jazz. George Antheil, writing for a German periodical, insisted that "jazz is not a craze. It has existed in America for the last hundred years and continues to exist each year more potently than the last. As for its artistic significance, the organization of its line, and color, its new dimensions, its new dynamics and mechanics—its significance is that it is one of the greatest landmarks of modern art."

The tendency became more and more to consider it seriously as an artistic force. A few months after Whiteman's concert a jazz symposium was held in Boston conducted by Professor Edward Burlingame Hill of Harvard University, and a conference on jazz was conducted by the League of Composers in New York. Mrs. Charles S. Guggenheimer was quoted as having said that a chair of American music devoted to the study and development of jazz was likely to be established at the American Academy of Rome; this prediction was unfortunately never realized. Less than two decades later, however, a serious course on jazz was given by the New School for Social Research in New York. But by that time jazz had ceased to be a curiosity—to be discussed, debated, praised and excoriated. It had achieved its accepted place of importance in American culture, the place that Paul Whiteman had always known it deserved.

CHAPTER SEVEN

GEORGE GERSHWIN

"I Got Rhythm . . . ."

GEORGE GERSHWIN

♪

GEORGE GERSHWIN

The evolution of jazz as we now know it owes as formidable a debt to the music of George Gershwin as it does to Paul Whiteman's performances. It might even be said, without detracting from Whiteman's contributions, that, but for having Gershwin's music as an ally, the bandleader's battle for the emancipation of jazz would have been much more prolonged; would have encountered much greater opposition; and his victory would possibly have been less decisive. The success of Whiteman's program was after all assured by its *pièce de résistance:* the *Rhapsody in Blue.* That masterpiece—and, for all its shortcomings, it *is* a masterpiece—gave Whiteman's concert point and meaning. It was the beacon shining a finger of light toward the future and destiny of jazz music.

Few musical compositions of our time have enjoyed the instantaneous triumph of the Gershwin work. The *Rhapsody,* wrote an editor of *Musical Courier,* Henry O. Osgood, "is a more important contribution to music than Stravinsky's *Rites of Spring.* To Deems Taylor it revealed a "genuine melodic gift and a piquant individual harmonic sense to lend significance to its rhythmic ingenuity. . . . It is genuine jazz music not only in its scoring but in its idiom." "Mr. Gershwin," reported W. J. Henderson, "has an irre-

119

pressible pack of talents and there is an element of inevitability about his piece." And Henry T. Finck insisted that Gershwin was "far superior to Schönberg, Milhaud, and the rest of the futurist fellows."

Such a critical accolade forecast the greater acclaim to come. It soon became the most famous piece of serious music by an American, and earned fabulous royalties. It was performed by jazz bands and symphony orchestras, by solo pianists, two-piano teams, and piano ensembles; by harmonica bands and mandolin orchestras; by tap dancers and ballet dancers; by choral groups. It was featured in stage shows and on the talking screen. It lent its principal theme to a novel, and furnished the signature for Paul Whiteman's radio shows.

Its success was easily understandable. Exciting music at first hearing, it proved even more so with familiarity. It was dramatic, emotional, lyric, rhapsodic. It had the appeal of novelty: it was the first major attempt to write jazz seriously within a large form. It was as native in its flavor as corn-on-the-cob, or a hot-dog, or a Manhattan cocktail; as intrinsically a product of American resourcefulness and imagination as the tabloid and the skyscraper, as engagingly informal as the strip-tease. It was something in which every American could find something of himself and his background; it was inevitable that Americans should respond to it enthusiastically.

But even many of those who praised the *Rhapsody* extravagantly in 1924 did not at first believe that it was much more than an intriguing pioneer work, destined for a short (if exciting) life. How many of its most passionate sponsors, searching their hearts for their most honest convictions, would have believed that the *Rhapsody* would still be alive twenty years thence? Or, much more, that it would remain the most frequently performed American symphonic work in the repertoire, to be conducted by Dmitri Mitropoulos and Toscanini, and performed by such artists as Iturbi and Sanromá?

The truth is that while many of us acclaimed the *Rhapsody* in 1924 for its charm, originality, and native traits, few of us realized how truly important this music really was. Those of us who had spent a lifetime in concert hall and conservatory were somewhat pedantically disconcerted by its technical lapses. It was, we had to confess, a poorly co-ordinated work; some of its harmonic structures were awkward; it failed to show a capacity to develop and enlarge thematic material imaginatively. We were right about those faults—they strike us anew each time we hear the work. But what we failed to realize at the time was that the *Rhapsody* had qualities that no deficiencies in technique could kill; and the most important of these qualities was its vitality. The music was alive, freshly conceived, put down on paper with enthusiasm and spontaneity. That vitality is still the most engaging trait of the work. Because it was born of inspiration, it defied the fumbling technique and the inexperience of its composer. Its youthful spirit, its contagious appeal, its cogency and power asserted themselves despite an incompetent structure. They still assert themselves today, even after a hundredth hearing of the work, and still magnetize us.

GEORGE GERSHWIN   121

What is true specifically of the *Rhapsody* is also true of Gershwin in general. Gershwin died in 1937. It can be said that he has become even more important after his death than he was in his lifetime. However much he was praised by critics and serious musicians when he was alive, such praise was inevitably tempered with reservations. Derive the common denominator of most criticisms received by Gershwin during his lifetime and it will probably prove to be as follows: He *was* talented; he exerted an influence; his music was both entertaining and exciting—but both he and his music were of ephemeral importance.

A handful of years, obviously, is too short a period to measure anyone's posthumous importance. But one thing is already reasonably certain about Gershwin's: it is by no means ephemeral. All-Gershwin programs, whether in the concert hall or over the radio, were pleasing novelties when Gershwin was alive; today they have become something of a ritual, over them hovering the aura of a shrine. Today, these concerts are growing more numerous, and are attracting larger audiences than several years ago—and one might add hastily, they never lacked popular appeal. The stature of Gershwin's music has grown perceptibly. The *Rhapsody* is permanently entrenched in the symphonic repertory. *Porgy and Bess* was only mildly accepted when it was first performed in 1935; most critics dismissed it as neither fish nor fowl, neither opera nor musical comedy. Since Gershwin's death it has won the David Bispham Silver Medal as the most important American achievement in the field of opera; it has been revived on Broadway to enjoy the longest run ever known by any revival in America; and it was singled out by the Music Critics Circle in New York as the most important musical revival of the year. Beyond all this, the melodies of *Porgy and Bess* proved to have such artistic merit that in 1943 they were combined by Robert Russell Bennett into an excellent symphonic suite which was performed by the New York Philharmonic and the Pittsburgh Symphony Orchestras.

When Gershwin was alive we accepted the fact that he was a force in music—particularly for his successful pioneer effort in using the jazz idiom in larger forms of serious music. Consciously or unconsciously, composers throughout the world were to be inspired by him to write works of their own in the jazz idiom. Maurice Ravel wrote a "blues" sonata. Ernst Křenek and Kurt Weill wrote jazz operas. Constant Lambert and William Walton wrote jazz symphonic suites. John Alden Carpenter wrote a jazz ballet. Aaron Copland wrote a jazz piano concerto. It is doubtful if jazz would have been accepted so openly in the polite society of the world's great composers if Gershwin had not first made a lady of her. As Walter Damrosch wrote picturesquely: "Various composers have been walking around jazz like a cat around a plate of hot soup, waiting for it to cool off so that they could enjoy it without burning their tongues, hitherto accustomed only to the more tepid liquid distilled by cooks of the classical school. Lady Jazz, adorned with her intriguing rhythms, has danced her way around the world. . . . But for all her travels and her sweeping popularity she has encountered no knight who could lift her to a level that would enable her to be received as a respectable member in musical circles. George Gershwin seems to have accomplished this miracle. He has done it boldly by dressing this extremely independent and up-to-date young lady in the classic garb. . . . Yet he has not detracted one whit from her fascinating personality. He is the Prince who has taken Cinderella by the hand and openly proclaimed her a princess to the astonished world, no doubt to the fury of her envious sisters."

What we could hardly be sure of during Gershwin's lifetime, but are today clearly realizing, is that no technical shortcomings can doom his works to oblivion. There have been American works boasting technical adroitness and elegant workmanship which have long since been forgotten, and which indeed never had even a temporary popularity. Their fate was obscurity because they had neither the inspiration nor the vitality that George Gershwin had. His melodic material is almost invariably interesting, sometimes for its dash and energy, sometimes for its warm and intoxicating lyricism; fired with the spark of true genius, these melodic ideas still glow, warming us each time we listen to them. His rhythmic patterns are often subtly ingenious, and endow his music with an irresistible dynamism. At its best, his music has mobility, rarely lapsing into monotony, invariably charged with high tensions and alive with electric currents. He had variety of touch; he could be witty, satiric, dramatic, introspective, tender, or hilarious. Most important of all, he spoke an American language, and with it he succeeded in creating an authentically American art.

George Gershwin, who was born in Brooklyn, New

York, on September 26, 1898, was no child prodigy. He was a typical American boy who delighted in the games of the street and in the companionship of other boys like himself. He liked to roller-skate, to play "cat," hockey, and punchball, to discuss the exploits of the baseball heroes of the day. He was not particularly adept at school work. He was not interested in books of any kind. For a while he looked with superior scorn upon any boy who had an even remote connection with music. Music was for "Maggies," he would say. At the age of six, however, he was fascinated by Rubinstein's *Melody in F*, which he heard in a penny arcade; and when he was nine he fell in love with a girl because she could sing. Yet, in spite of such experiences, he refused to consider his musical interest seriously.

He was about ten years old when he became fully awakened to music. He was attending Public School 25, on the Lower East Side, where one of his fellow pupils was a talented young violinist named Maxie Rosenzweig (later to be known on the concert stage as Max Rosen). Maxie gave a concert in the public auditorium which George—still contemptuous of music and those who pursued it—refused to attend. Instead he played ball in the schoolyard. While he was running around, he heard the strains of Maxie's violin in Dvořák's *Humoresque*. In spite of himself, George stopped playing ball, drew closer to the open window, and listened. That music made so deep an impression on him that he was determined to become a friend of the violinist. For a few hours he stood outside the school building (oblivious of the rain), hoping to catch Maxie on his way home. Then, having missed him, he discovered Maxie's address and went straight to his home.

There he told Maxie how much his violin-playing meant to him. And they became friends.

Maxie's influence on George was profound. He revealed to the younger boy the undreamed-of world of great music. He told him stories of the great composers, and George listened spellbound. He played for George from the violin repertoire. From then on the streets lost their fascination for the boy; he had found music, and it became his only pleasure. One day, on discovering a piano in the house of a friend, he immediately started to experiment with the keys. Soon he picked up some of the rudiments of piano-playing and with that knowledge began to compose some fragmentary tunes. These he exhibited to his friend with the diffident pride of a doting father.

"I'm sorry," Maxie told him. "You haven't got any talent for music. You'd better forget all about it."

But George could no longer "forget about" music; it had become an inextricable part of him. When his family acquired a piano he continued to study, first by himself, then with some inadequate teachers. And he continued to write pieces of his own—pieces in imitation of the popular tunes of the day.

3.

Gershwin's career from the very first was marked by a passionate ideal to bring musical significance to American popular music. Even as an adolescent, he saw his goal clearly—though, to be sure, he groped blindly to find the right path toward it. Deep within him, he always felt that he had a mission to perform;

the performance of that mission was the guiding force of his entire life.

When, as a boy, he studied the piano with Charles Hambitzer, his first important teacher, he would argue tirelessly about the value of popular music. Hambitzer looked upon the American popular song contemptuously, as every trained musician did at the time. But George—sensitive though he was to Chopin and Debussy, as revealed to him by Hambitzer—was fascinated by the popular idiom. "Alexander's Ragtime Band," then a nationwide hit, excited him, and in a far different way from the masters. It was something personal to *him*, the kind of music he wanted to write when he knew how. Indefatigably he would try to transmit his own enthusiasm to his teacher, to make Hambitzer hear these songs with his own ears and to react to them with his own enthusiasms.

"I have a new pupil who will make a mark in music if anybody will," Hambitzer wrote prophetically to his sister at the time. "The boy is a genius, without a doubt; he's just crazy about music and can't wait until it is time to take his lesson. No watching the clock for this boy! He wants to go in for this modern stuff, jazz and what not. But I'm not going to let him for a while. I'll see that he gets a firm foundation in the standard music first."

It was because, almost from the beginning of his career, Gershwin was fired with the mission of making the American popular song artistically valid that he searched restlessly in the music of the masters for direction. When, during his adolescent years, he worked as a hack pianist in Tin Pan Alley, he spent several weeks dissecting Bach's *Well-Tempered Clavier* for a key to its structure. Somewhat later he joined the harmony class of Rubin Goldmark. Throughout his life he talked about escaping from contractual obligations and the uninterrupted pressure of life in Manhattan, to devote himself to intensive study. One of the major reasons for his trip to Europe in 1928 was to realize this desire. Europe, unfortunately, merely duplicated the pressures and obligations of New York, and study there was as impossible as it had been in America. However, a few years before his death, he began comprehensive technical study with the late Joseph Schillinger of New York, and then applied himself to his studies with the industry and application of a conscientious schoolboy.

Though he early realized fame and fortune as a composer of popular songs, his perspective was not distorted. His artistic compulsions were too strong to be satisfied merely with the applause of the masses, and the financial rewards for satisfying them. It was more important for him to fulfill the destiny of jazz. "I regard jazz as an American folk music," he wrote during the height of his success, expressing a lifelong conviction; "a very powerful one which is probably in the blood of the American people more than any other style of folk music. I believe that it can be made the basis of serious symphonic works of lasting value."*

"Jazz," he wrote again, "is music; it uses the same notes that Bach used. When jazz is played in another country it is called American. It is a very energetic kind of music; noisy, boisterous, and even vulgar. One

* George Gershwin, "The Relation of Jazz to American Music," *American Composers on American Music*, edited by Henry Cowell. (Stanford University Press, 1933).

thing is certain: jazz has contributed an enduring value to American achievement in the sense that it has expressed us. It is an original American achievement which will endure—not in jazz, perhaps—but which will leave its mark on future music in one form or another."*

His ambitions made it impossible for him to yield to the temptation to which so many other popular song composers succumbed—contenting himself with formulas and clichés. He had achieved success early in life. He published his first song when he was eighteen years old: "When You Want 'Em You Can't Get 'Em," which was accepted by Harry von Tilzer and earned five dollars for its proud composer. By the time he was twenty, he had produced a smash hit—"Swanee"—which sold millions of copies of sheet music and records. When he was twenty-two he was writing music for George White's *Scandals* (one of the most desirable assignments on Broadway), and his songs were interpolated in numerous other Broadway productions, some of them featuring such stars as Irene Bordoni and Ed Wynn. Even London had ordered a score from him for one of its major musical productions.

Such immediate recognition—and the wealth it brought with it—might have turned many a head, and sent into the discard more than one ideal. But Gershwin never lost sobriety, or the ability to analyze himself and his purpose. He did not forget the goal he had set both for himself and for jazz. Other composers, in the face of such successes, might easily have been tempted into imitating and repeating the manner and

*George Gershwin, "The Composer in the Machine Age," in *Revolt in the Arts,* edited by Oliver M. Saylor. (New York: Coward-McCann, 1933).

style which had caught a nation's fancy. But the public's acclaim—pleasurable though it proved to be—was with Gershwin a lesser consideration. Because he wanted to write good jazz music, he brushed aside his early efforts impatiently, however successful they may have been with the public. He knew what he wanted: a fluid melody that had freshness of feeling and originality of line and design; subtle rhythmic effects; rich harmonic colors, of original tints and hues. He wanted his songs to be marked by an inevitability of structure in which no note or phrase was superfluous. He wanted an idiom that would be both popular and original. And he worked hard—probably no popular song composer worked more painstakingly than he. He revised every line and phrase and nuance dozens of times. Many songs were discarded as incomplete realizations of his ideals. Occasionally he achieved a momentary felicitousness of expression that made him realize that he was not slaving in vain, and that, though he was groping, he was at least groping in the right direction.

By 1924 he had written several songs which satisfied him. There was "I'll Build a Stairway to Paradise" from the *Scandals of 1922*, with its suave and well-polished manner and its neatness of construction; "Do It Again" from *The French Doll* in which the touch was intriguingly deft; "Somebody Loves Me" from the *Scandals of 1924*, with its enchanting lyric line given piquancy by the injection of the blues note; "Oh, Lady, Be Good" from *Lady Be Good*, with its rhythmic drive. With such songs he was becoming a master of his tools, and he was using these tools to fashion songs that were his personal handiwork. In these songs a high degree of compositorial skill was combined with a flair for original melody, with a capacity to project subtle suggestions of mood and feelings, with a dynamism of irresistible drive, with a spice of idiom.

4.

A handful of farsighted and discerning musicians recognized the gleams of genius in these songs. In Tin Pan Alley Gershwin's stoutest advocates included Max Dreyfus, Irving Berlin, and Jerome Kern—and their praise was unqualified. But even outside of Tin Pan Alley there were those who took note of what he was doing.

One of these was the American pianist and composer Beryl Rubinstein, who startled a newspaper interviewer by speaking of Gershwin as a "great" composer. No one before this had ever dared to attribute "greatness" to a composer of popular songs. "I am absolutely earnest," Rubinstein insisted. "This young fellow . . . has the spark of musical genius which is definite in his serious moods. . . . With Gershwin's style and seriousness he is not definitely of the popular music school, but is one of the really outstanding figures in this country's serious musical efforts. . . . This young man has great charm and a most magnetic personality, and I really believe that America will at no distant date honor him for his talent . . . and that when we speak of American composers, George Gershwin's name will be prominent on our list."

This interview took place in 1922—two years before *Rhapsody in Blue!* One year later another serious artist gave a bow of recognition to Gershwin. As has been told in the chapter on Whiteman, the singer Eva Gauthier included three Gershwin songs—"I'll Build a Stairway to Paradise," "Innocent Ingénue Baby," and "Swanee" (a fourth Gershwin song, "Do It Again," came as an encore)—on a program devoted to great vocal music. This was the first time that jazz songs had been heard at a dignified recital, and it was appropriate that they had been brought there by Gershwin.

This book has already described Paul Whiteman's enthusiasm for Gershwin. He had been playing Gershwin melodies since 1920 and had found them to be the kind of jazz expression for which he himself was striving in his performances. A bond of friendship and mutual admiration developed between the two musicians. In 1923 Whiteman and his orchestra were in the pit of George White's *Scandals,* for which Gershwin had written all the music. One of the novelties of that production was a one-act Negro opera entitled *135th Street.* This opera was dropped from the revue after only one performance because George White felt that it was too gloomy for Broadway audiences. But Whiteman, as he conducted it during rehearsals and at its initial presentation, was convinced that its composer was destined for greater spheres than that of the popular song. In *135th Street*—for all its unevenness, self-consciousness, and occasional naïveté—there was an unmistakable native flavor that Whiteman had found in few American works, and that suggested to him *how* jazz might be used as an idiom in serious music.

When Whiteman planned his historic concert of

jazz music at Aeolian Hall to draw the attention of the world of music to the importance of jazz, he hoped to feature on his program a major jazz work written expressly for the occasion. Unhesitatingly his mind went to Gershwin. Gershwin required a great deal of persuasion, for he felt that he was not yet ready for a major assignment. But Whiteman was intransigent, and his flow of arguments and entreaties was irresistible.

The idea for his work occurred to Gershwin late in 1923.* "There had been so much talk about the limitations of jazz, not to speak of the manifest misunderstanding of its function," Gershwin told an interviewer. "Jazz, they said, had to be in strict time. It had to cling to dance rhythms. I resolved, if possible, to kill that misconception with one sturdy blow. Inspired by this aim, I set to composing. I had no set plan, no structure, to which my music could conform. The *Rhapsody*, you see, began as a purpose, not a plan. I worked out a few themes, but just at this time I had to appear in Boston for the première of *Sweet Little Devil*. It was on the train, with its steely rhythms, its rattly-bang that is so often stimulating to a composer, that I suddenly heard—even saw on paper—the complete construction of the *Rhapsody* from beginning to end. No new themes came to me, but I worked on the thematic material already in my mind, and tried to conceive the composition as a whole. I heard it as a sort of musical kaleidoscope of America—of our vast melting pot, of our incomparable national pep, our blues, our metropolitan madness. By the time I reached

* The frequently printed story to the effect that the *Rhapsody in Blue* was composed in three weeks has been proved legendary.

Boston, I had the definite plot of the piece, as distinguished from its actual substance.

"The middle theme came upon me suddenly, as my music often does. It was at the home of a friend, just as I got back to Gotham. I must do a great deal of what you might call subconscious composing, and this is an example. Playing at parties is one of my notorious weaknesses. As I was playing, without a thought of the *Rhapsody,* all at once I heard myself playing a theme that must have been haunting me inside, seeking outlet. No sooner had it oozed out of my fingers than I realized I had found it. Within a week of my return from Boston I had completed the structure in the rough of the *Rhapsody in Blue.*"

Revision required several weeks of detailed work. It is said that Gershwin was still working on melodic and harmonic details when the composition went into rehearsal. Then the manuscript was passed on to Ferde Grofé for orchestration.* The story goes—and there are those who testify to its authenticity—that at the first rehearsal of the *Rhapsody,* Whiteman was so affected by the music that he forgot to beat time and instead listened enthralled. As the beautiful lyric section progressed, his baton fell from his hand, and he was trembling. "Damn that fellow!" Whiteman is quoted as having said after the rehearsal. "Did he actually think he could improve it?" At the concert Whiteman was even more deeply moved by the music. "Somewhere in the middle of the score," he confessed, "I began crying. When I came to myself, I was eleven pages along, and to this day I cannot tell you how I conducted that far."

* On all his large works subsequent to the *Rhapsody,* Gershwin did his own orchestration.

5.

After the *Rhapsody in Blue,* Gershwin consolidated his position as America's leading—and favorite—composer. For the Broadway theater he wrote one excellent score after another for musical comedies which generally proved to be among the leading successes of their respective seasons. In this field he profited no end from the collaboration with his brother Ira, who provided the songs with deft and skillfully contrived lyrics. *Tip Toes* (1925), *Oh Kay* (1926), *Strike Up the Band* (1927), *Rosalie* (1927), *Funny Face* (1927), *Treasure Girl* (1928), *Show Girl* (1929), *Girl Crazy* (1930)—these were but the prelude to the crowning success of his theatrical career, the political satire *Of Thee I Sing* (1931) which became the first musical comedy ever to win the Pulitzer Prize. During these same years he was writing serious works as well—works that were also in the jazz idiom, magnificently proving that the *Rhapsody* had been no mere flash in the pan: *Concerto in F* for piano and orchestra (1925), *Jazz Piano Preludes* (1926), *An American in Paris* (1928), *Second Rhapsody* (1931), *Cuban Overture* (1934), and the opera *Porgy and Bess* (1935).

He won for himself wealth, fame, the adoration of the masses, and the admiration of many world-famous composers and critics. "Who could ask for anything more?" Yet he remained, in spite of the seemingly endless parade of triumphs, a modest and highly self-critical young man. Simple and wholesome in all things (he never forgot that he had been raised on the East Side, and his penthouse never inspired any delusions of grandeur), he viewed his music with healthy detachment. If he was proud of it—and he was, with a pride that led him to perform it at the slightest provocation anywhere and everywhere—he was also critical of it. He was ever conscious of his technical shortcomings and lamented them. He had, as a matter of fact, the exaggerated awe for schoolbook learning that only the unschooled have. He always acknowledged that he still had far to go to achieve status as a serious composer. In short, though he loved his music, he underestimated both it and the capacity of his talent to overcome inadequacy of technique. It was difficult to make him realize that his best songs had a greatness which not all the conservatory learning in the world could have enhanced, that his instincts and taste guided his hand as surely as any set rules could have done. It was even more difficult to convince him that the technical faults of his larger works were comparatively unimportant. What *was* important was his wonderful exuberance, his melodic richness, his native talent.

It is silly to say—as some have said—that Gershwin in his larger works would not have been the better for a sound technique. But the lack of it could not debar him from greatness. His melodic sense was as highly sensitized as that of any trained musician. His instinct dictated his use of subtle modulations, ingenious shifting accents, which lent a touch of magic to the best of his songs. "The Man I Love," "Soon," "Embraceable You," "Someone to Watch Over Me"—these, though "popular songs," are far from negligible; in their own way they proved quite as emphatically as did his larger works that jazz could be made *good music*.

It is interesting to note that Europe has been far less concerned than we over the flaws in Gershwin's larger works. In spite of the racy American speech of his music, Europe has acclaimed it. The *Rhapsody* and the *Concerto* have been performed by many major orchestras in Europe, and the *Rhapsody* was interpreted by ballets in Paris and London. In July, 1931, *An American in Paris* was given an ovation at the International Society for Contemporary Music, meeting that year in London. In Italy, shortly before his death, Gershwin was elected an honorary member of the St. Cecilia Academy of Music in Rome—the highest honor that can be accorded a foreign composer. Even in Nazi Germany, Gershwin's music—supposedly tabu because its composer was a Jew—has been heard in high places. Countess Waldeck, in her book, *Athene Palace,* quotes an important Nazi official as confessing: "Do you know there is not one of us who has not a Gershwin record in the bottom of a drawer, which he plays sometimes late at night?"

6.

Gershwin's greatest work was his last, the opera *Porgy and Bess,* an earnest of his ever-ripening creative powers. He had been searching for a suitable opera libretto for some time before he finally came upon and selected the play of Du Bose Heyward presented by the Theater Guild. A story of Negro life in Charleston's Catfish Row, *Porgy* appeared to Gershwin ideally suited for American operatic treatment.

Once he had decided on the libretto, the opera obsessed him. He brushed aside about a quarter of a million dollars' worth of contracts to devote himself exclusively to his new work. He sketched the broad outlines. Then, feeling the need for personal acquaintance with Negro life and authentic Negro music, he spent several weeks in and near Charleston. He heard, and studied, the street cries of the peddlers; he saturated himself with every Negro idiom heard in the vicinity of Charleston; he even participated in an actual "shout" of the Gullahs, and later improvised a "shout" of his own. Then, having assimilated Negro music, he set to work on his opera. The writing of the score took him eleven months; orchestration required an additional nine months. Directed by Rouben Mamoulian and conducted by Alexander Smallens, *Porgy and Bess* was presented by the Theater Guild, first in Boston, on the evening of September 30, 1935, then two weeks later at the Alvin Theater in New York.

The reaction to the new opera was at the time generally unfavorable. It has required the perspective of a few years to realize what Gershwin actually accomplished. He had written a folk opera in the vein of Moussorgsky, with broad strokes of realism blended with touches of pure poetry. It was not an opera in the traditional definition of the term—but then neither was *Boris Godunov*. It was a folk tale, told with directness and in indigenous American accents. The music, as well as the book, projected Negro humor and pathos, nobility and savagery, mellow wisdom and naïveté, without resorting to caricature. It was a portrait of a race, drawn with majestic strokes.

It is a reflection of Gershwin's artistry that, though he did not quote a single phrase of authentic Negro music, his score should have the quality of Negro folk lore. He had so saturated himself in Charleston with the Negro idiom that when he wrote his music it acquired an unmistakably racial character. He had captured in his music the atmosphere of Catfish Row. His street cries, his "shouts," his spiritual-like lamentations, sound as if they had been written by a generation of oppressed Negroes, and yet every single note was his own.

In this score he was the mature composer whose command of expression had an extraordinarily wide gamut from the lyric to the dramatic, from the burlesque to the tragic. Here he was a master of the jazz idiom, making it serve his every purpose—his servant rather than his master.

There was demonstrated here—as there had been elsewhere—his wonderful melodic gift: "Summertime" and "I Got Plenty of Nuttin' " represent Gershwin at his lyric best. Here, too, was a deft use of rhythm and dissonance to inject the spice of humor. But with this, a much richer and deeper note was heard—a note for which we had been searching in vain in his earlier works. That note sounds loud and clear in the Wake Scene and in the closing moments of the opera, revealing a great creative artist arriving at the height of his powers. It was in such passages that Gershwin indicated how truly far he might have traveled had he lived to fulfill his rich promise.

7.

After completing *Porgy and Bess,* Gershwin went to Hollywood to write music for the screen—his second visit to the movie capital, and his first since 1931. He now wrote scores for a Fred Astaire-Ginger Rogers musical, *Shall We Dance;* for a second Astaire film, *A Damsel in Distress,* and for a lavish musical produced by Samuel Goldwyn, *The Goldwyn Follies.*

It was while he was working on this last film that, suddenly and without warning, he collapsed in his studio. It was at first believed that he had been suffering from the strain of overwork. But a second attack, a few weeks later, betrayed the symptoms of a brain tumor. An effort was made to procure the services of a famous Eastern surgeon, Dr. Walter E. Danby, but Danby felt that the condition was far too serious to warrant waiting until he could fly to the Coast. Therefore, at the Cedars of Lebanon Hospital in Hollywood, Dr. Carl Rand removed a cystic tumor from the right temporal lobe of the brain. But the operation had come too late. On the morning of July 11, 1937, George Gershwin died. His brother, Ira, was with him until the very end.

Expressions of grief were sounded over the radio and in the press; there were tributes to Gershwin from America's leading musicians, and all-Gershwin concerts were organized from New York to Hollywood. Four days after his death, the funeral service—at Temple Emanu-El in New York—was attended by more than three thousand of Gershwin's admirers, representing leaders from every walk of life. The honorary pall-bearers included Mayor LaGuardia, ex-Mayor James J. Walker, George M. Cohan, Walter Damrosch, and Edwin Franko Goldman. Following the musical program—which included Bach and Beethoven as well as the lyric section from the *Rhapsody in Blue*—Rabbi Stephen S. Wise delivered the eulogy.

But what might most aptly serve as a fitting epitaph was spoken by Eva Gauthier—the same Eva Gauthier who had been the first artist to perform Gershwin's music in a concert hall: "George Gershwin will live as long as music lives. . . . He will never be forgotten, and his place will never be filled."

CHAPTER EIGHT

JEROME KERN
RODGERS AND HART
COLE PORTER

"I've Got The Tune . . . ."

JEROME KERN

♪

JEROME KERN

It was Jerome Kern's music that first proved to young Gershwin that he was not succumbing to an idle dream in envisioning an artistic future for the popular song. When he was sixteen he attended his aunt's wedding at the Grand Central Hotel, and during the evening the band struck up a melody that captivated him instantly. It was excitingly original in melodic structure, and richly clever in harmonic and rhythmic details. When it was finished, George rushed to the bandstand to ask for its title. It was the song "You're Here and I'm Here" from a musical comedy by Jerome Kern. George begged for other numbers by the same composer, and the bandleader played another Kern song, "They Didn't Believe Me."

From that moment on Kern became for Gershwin a great source of inspiration and at times a model for imitation. It is even said that Gershwin (having discovered Kern's address) would stand for hours under his window with the hope of hearing him play his songs at the piano. "I studied Kern and I imitated him," Gershwin frequently confessed. "Many of the songs I wrote at that time sounded exactly like his."

2.

With Jerome Kern a relatively unfamiliar kind of

composer entered Tin Pan Alley. Here was no illiterate musician, able to play in only one key on the piano and forced to dictate his tunes to an amanuensis. Here was, instead, a well-trained musician who had mastered the compositorial technique and who consciously enriched his songs through that flexible use of tonality, harmony, and rhythm which can come only after intensive preparatory training. What had fascinated Gershwin in those early Kern songs—and what had been so rare in the popular music of the day—was the intriguing changes of tempo, the occasional modulation, the enrichment of harmonic background which opened up new horizons to the popular song.

When, in 1910, Kern was assigned his first Broadway task—to rewrite the score for a New York show called *Mr. Wix of Wickham*—he had decided at once to put his best foot forward. He brought to this task not only his melodic inventiveness, in which he has never been lacking, but also his conservatory training in harmony and counterpoint—a mysterious science of which most Broadway composers at that time were sublimely innocent. The result was a soundly musical and an ingeniously contrived score which inspired one critic—the famous Alan Dale—to inquire: "Who is this Jerome Kern, whose music towers in an Eiffel way above the average primitive hurdy-gurdy accompaniment of the present-day musical comedy?"

With his very first undertaking on Broadway, Kern had thus impressed his talent and musicianship upon a few discerning people. It was not long before he impressed them upon large audiences as well. In 1911 he wrote his first original score for Broadway, *The Red Petticoat*, and—while it was not an outstanding success

—there were those who remarked that the music was unusually good. Three years later, in *The Girl from Utah*, he produced his first smash song hit—a wistful, poignant tune sung by Julia Sanderson, called "They Didn't Believe Me." From this time on Kern became one of the busiest of Broadway composers. Hardly a season passed without Kern music for some important production; occasionally two or three were heard in the same season. Between 1915 and 1919 alone he was responsible for the music of at least nineteen productions.

3.

Jerome Kern would like you to believe that he became a composer largely through the accident of having once proved himself to be a poor businessman. He was seventeen years old at the time, a student of music at the New York College of Music. He knew what he wanted: some more study (preferably in Europe), and then a career as a composer of popular music. But his father insisted that he enter his merchandising establishment in Newark as a prelude to a life as a middle-class businessman. Kern agreed because there was no alternative: his father simply would not listen to his argument that there was a future for him in music.

One of Kern's first business deals involved the purchase of two pianos in New York City. Young Kern returned to Newark to confess to his father somewhat diffidently that he had been induced to buy not two, but two hundred, pianos. His father required no further convincing that the boy belonged not to business but to music.

Kern says that he bought the two hundred pianos instead of the specified two because he had been guileless and simple, easily persuaded by soft words and an affable manner. But in the light of some other Kern experiences of a later day, there are some who wonder if there was not at the time a good deal of method in his madness. After all, with that one deal—much more eloquently than with a barrage of arguments—he had been able to persuade his father to let him turn exclusively to music. This fact alone (not even considering the subsequent fact—that his father actually made a handsome profit by selling those pianos on the installment plan!) makes his blunder assume the guise of a major maneuver.

Are we ascribing to Kern a subtlety of machination of which he, a kid of seventeen, was altogether innocent? Perhaps . . . but other, later events warrant a faint doubt. Take, for example, the matter of his passion for book-collecting. He has always been an inveterate collector of one thing or another, and at one time his collecting mania was concentrated on rare books and first editions. For years the word passed from one bookseller to the next that a full-grown sucker had sprung up in their midst in the person of a successful popular song composer. Kern (very much like the Oscar Wilde cynic who knew the value of everything but the price of nothing) seemed to buy every first edition in sight, rarely quibbling over the fancy prices asked. Behind his back booksellers laughed at this sweet and expensive innocence. Innocence, indeed! Only a few years later the same booksellers scrambled over one another in their mad haste to buy these very same books, paying the aggregate sum of $1,729,000, or almost twice as much as the books had cost Kern. And—if this were not enough to give Kern the last laugh—there was the additional striking fact that the auction took place late in 1928: exactly a year before the economic holocaust that was to devastate the book market (along with many another booming business) to such a point that Kern's collection would then have brought in hardly a tenth of what it had sold for before the crash.

It may be that his book-collecting *had* become (as Kern himself explained) such a responsibility and a problem that selling it was essential to his peace of mind. That he disposed of it a year before the Blue Monday of 1929 may well have been—as Kern insists— just a happy stroke of luck. It may also be true that the reason Kern abandoned the stock market early in 1929, selling all his securities at top prices, was merely that he had suddenly tired of the whole business. Obviously, in both cases, Kern could not have known or guessed that an economic crash of epic proportions was just around the corner. Yet it seems just a little too happy a chance that he should have sold both his stocks and his valuable books at the zero hour, just as it seems a little too happy a chance that he should have made a disastrous business coup many years earlier precisely in time to persuade his father to let him return to music. When lightning strikes persistently in the same place, one is perhaps justified in suspecting, not that the laws of probability have been suspended, but that there lurks in the vicinity an attracting agent.

Quietly unassuming, modest, shy, honest, unpretentious, Jerome Kern is likely to give a false impression of simplicity. He looks through his horn-rimmed glasses with an expression of innocence. He is mild-mannered, soft of voice, suggesting the traditional college professor rather than a man of the world who has won first place for himself in the two fiercely competitive worlds of Broadway and Hollywood.

But scratch the surface of ingenuousness and you come upon qualities more characteristically Kern: a sound instinct, a tireless industry, good sense, quiet self-assurance, and a remarkable capacity to size up a situation and take advantage of it. These have served him in whatever he has engaged himself in—he is nobody's fool. And particularly well have they served him in music.

He has extraordinary talent, of course: a vein of melody, tender and seductive, together with an ability to provide these melodies with harmonic settings of great variety and enchantment. But talent alone—however great—would not have kept him the top man in his field for more than three decades if it had not also been combined with hard-fisted shrewdness, penetrating judgment, and astuteness. The composer of scores for more than a hundred musical comedies (most of them successful) and a dozen Hollywood films, all of which produced a rich crop of songs incomparable for charm, Kern is second only to Irving Berlin as the oldest and most successful functioning composer of popular music of the past half-century. He first achieved success in 1911; by 1915 he was one of the most sought after composers for the Broadway theater. Today he is still in a class by himself, still eagerly demanded, still receiving staggering fees for his work. He has retained that success in spite of the changing styles in popular music from ragtime to swing—changing styles which have temporarily brought new gods to the fore and destroyed old ones. And he has retained his success without catering at any time to the fad of the hour, without sacrificing his own individuality or artistic integrity.

He has had the "breaks"—no doubt of that. No one can reach success as quickly and decisively as Kern did without some collaboration on the part of Dame Fortune. But "breaks" can hardly explain his long and uninterrupted reign over the popular music of our time; for this, you must credit his resourcefulness, his keen intuition, and acumen—these and his wonderful native gifts.

4.

Kern was born in New York City on January 27, 1885. His father, president of the Street Sprinkler's Association, had the concession for the watering of Manhattan's streets and was able to provide his family with a comfortable home. Jerome's mother, a lover of good music, initiated him (and his brothers) into piano-playing. Jerome Kern still recalls with no little nostalgic pleasure the eight-handed piano concerts which he gave in the Kern living room with his mother and two brothers. When he had outgrown his mother's instruction, he took further lessons with a girl in the neighborhood.

When Jerome was ten, his family moved to Newark where his father had acquired a merchandising house. At the Newark High School he played the organ for the assembly, wrote music for, and helped direct, the school shows. He did not care much for schoolwork or lessons, and was grateful to music for providing him with some avenue of escape. His academic studies came to an end when he left high school. He continued with his music, however, at the New York College of Music, where he was a pupil of Alexander Lambert and Paolo Gallico, and privately with Austin Pierce.

Every pupil at the College of Music talked of completing his music study in Europe, and Jerome was no exception. After his business deal as a member of his father's firm had cleared his way for further study, Kern made several trips to Europe, did some studying there, and held a variety of jobs (both here and abroad) which brought him into an ever closer relationship with his first love—popular music. In New York he got a job as pianist song-plugger with the Lyceum Publishing Company for seven dollars a week. His duties consisted of playing the piano in the city's large department stores, exploiting his publisher's lists; in this he was assisted—and how this does date him!—by two grand gentlemen of old Tin Pan Alley, Jean Schwartz and Ernest R. Ball. In London he found some work in the office of Charles Frohman, composing bits for the theater. London musicals at the time frequently used inexpensive pieces by unknown composers for their opening numbers, the theory being that audiences habitually came late anyway and did not hear them; the best music was reserved for the middle of the program. Kern was given several assignments to provide opening music. It cannot be said that he succeeded single-handed in changing the dilatory habits of London theater audiences, but he did get some favorable comment, and a great deal of experience which was soon to serve him in good stead in New York.

5.

Originality and resourcefulness won him a permanent place on the top in the New York theater, at the side of such established box-office favorites as Victor Herbert and Rudolph Friml. These same qualities kept him on top long after Herbert and Friml were displaced by other, and younger, men like Gershwin, Rodgers, Porter, and Youmans.

It required considerable vision (not to say courage) for a composer of such solid successes as *Sally, Sunny,* and a dozen other lavish musical comedies even to consider the possibility of writing a score for a book so unorthodox as Edna Ferber's *Show Boat.* In no other field of American arts, lively or otherwise, was change looked upon with greater horror than in musical comedy, in which tradition had dictated a form from which no one seemed capable of departing. The book—an excuse for chorus girls, lavish scenery, and set musical pieces—had become as formalized as a wedding ceremony; and the music with it. In view of this tradition a book like *Show Boat* was revolutionary. Edna Ferber herself thought Kern a bit quixotic in suggesting the conversion of her novel into a Broadway musical comedy. As she recalls in her autobiography: "When he suggested that I give him and Oscar Hammerstein the musical-dramatic rights in *Show Boat,* I thought he was being fantastic."

Miss Ferber has eloquently described her first reactions to Kern's score for *Show Boat:* "As the writing

JEROME KERN   153

of the musical play proceeded (and its ups and downs were even more heartbreaking than those of most musical plays), I heard bits and pieces of the score. Once or twice everything was seemingly abandoned because Ziegfeld said he couldn't produce the play. Almost a year went by. I had heard 'Can't Help Lovin' Dat Man' with its love-bemused lyric. I had melted under the bewitching strains of 'Make Believe' and 'Why Do I Love You?' and Gaylord Ravenal's insolent and careless gambler's song. And then Jerome Kern appeared at my apartment late one afternoon with a strange look of quiet exaltation in his eyes. He sat down at the piano. He doesn't play the piano particularly well and his singing voice, though true, is negligible. He played and sang 'Ol' Man River.' The music mounted, mounted, and I give you my word my hair stood on end, the tears came to my eyes, and I breathed like a heroine in a melodrama. This was great music. This was music that would outlast Jerome Kern's day and mine. I never have heard it since without that emotional surge."[*]

Show Boat, as finally produced by Ziegfeld at the Ziegfeld Theater on December 27, 1927, was not only revolutionary; it was also a gilt-edged investment. It ran for more than a year, grossing about fifty thousand dollars a week, was revived for a second successful run, and was sold several different times to the movies. If the critics called it our best folk operetta, the audiences called it grand entertainment and were refreshed, rather than upset, by its new treatment of musical-comedy materials.

[*] Edna Ferber, *A Peculiar Treasure* (New York: Doubleday, Doran & Company, 1939).

Unorthodoxy also marked some of Kern's later musical shows. *The Cat and the Fiddle* dispensed with chorus girls; musically it went even farther by introducing a fugue at one point. *Music in the Air*, written in the same sprightly vein as *The Cat and the Fiddle*, followed its predecessor in exploiting an unusual plot, and treating it with consistency and credibility. In both these musical comedies, as in *Show Boat*, many of the usual clichés of musical-comedy plot and structure were thrown overboard like so much jetsam. Musical writing acquired an incomparable richness of scope (incomparable, that is, for musical comedy) as well as greater independence. There are those who say that Jerome Kern was responsible for reviving the interest of jaded theater-goers in musical comedy at a moment when they were tiring of its lavishness and absurdities. This may go a step too far; but it isn't going too far to say that Kern, more than any other single person, injected an innovating spirit into an effete form of theatrical entertainment.

In 1931 he went to Hollywood to write the music for a film called *Men of the Sky*. He has since then assisted in filming some of his musical-comedy successes (including *Show Boat, Cat and the Fiddle, Music in the Air, Sunny,* and *Roberta*). Besides this he has written original scores for new films like *Swing Time* and *You Were Never Lovelier* (both with Fred Astaire); *High, Wide, and Handsome* and *Joy of Living* (both with Irene Dunne); *I Dream Too Much* (with Lily Pons), and several others which have helped not a little in setting a new standard for Hollywood music. One of his numbers from *Swing Time*—"The Way

You Look Tonight"—won the Academy Award in 1936 as the best screen song of the year.

He has since settled permanently in Beverly Hills, where he lives with his wife (a simple and frugal woman who governs the checkbook), his two grand pianos, and his collection of phonographs. It is a large and beautifully decorated house, but his favorite room is his studio, which is cluttered with books, music, and curios, and which—more often than not—is in disorder. Here he relaxes by reading a book or by smoking his pipe as he listens to the radio. Here he entertains his intimate friends. Here, too, he does his composing. When he is at work, a pipe is usually in his mouth, and a jar of candy at his right hand—as he alternates between smoking and munching on sweets. Frequently the radio is playing full-blast—though his concentration is so deep that he is oblivious to it.

Though he now lives in Hollywood and is so intimately associated with the screen, his heart belongs to Broadway. The living theater inebriates him. This usually mild fellow, with his soft eyes and gentle manner, becomes transfigured backstage. Even his dress (usually staid and undemonstrative) acquires new splashes of garish color; he discards his street clothes for vividly colored slacks and shirts, as if to point up the change of personality. He becomes nervous, irritable—a dynamo of energy. No phase of the production eludes his critical eye; he is always there with suggestions as to plot, acting, staging, lighting. In the midst of all this frenetic activity, a new melody may occur to him; then he will summon everyone in sight—from the leading lady to the scrubwoman washing the floors —and play the tune for them, asking their opinion.

The funny thing, too, is that he takes their verdict very seriously.

It is because the theater galvanizes Kern that he has been able to do his best composing for it. As a matter of fact, he finds it difficult to produce a song isolated from a dramatic text; his hit "The Last Time I Saw Paris" was exceptional. Working with a text, he is capable of incomparable productiveness—he practically sweats melodies. But he is a careful worker, a methodical craftsman, who revises his tunes many times before he is completely satisfied with them. Some of his best songs have originated as a result of a moment's happy inspiration, but in the end are the result of fastidious carving. He works over the details—harmonic as well as melodic—with the painstaking care of a composer writing a large work; yet the final product has a wonderful feeling of spontaneity, of having been written in one piece and in white heat: "Look for the Silver Lining," "Ol' Man River," "Why Do I Love You?," "Smoke Gets in Your Eyes," "They Didn't Believe Me," "All the Things You Are," "The Song Is You," "The Way You Look Tonight," and some hundred others.

Kern by no means looks disparagingly upon the popular song form. Rather, he considers it an important medium for a creative artist. And the world at large has responded by giving his songs serious consideration, and by assigning to them a status of artistic respectability. Concert singers like Lily Pons, Paul Robeson, and John Charles Thomas have sung his songs. "The Way You Look Tonight" and "The Song Is You" have been taken into the repertoire of the Gordon String Quartet in special chamber-music arrangements. An orchestral suite from *Show Boat* (*Scenario for Orchestra*) was introduced by the Cleveland Orchestra under Artur Rodzinski, and subsequently enjoyed almost a hundred performances by most of the major American orchestras. "Ol' Man River" has been accepted by many musicians as worthy of classification with Negro spirituals.

Occasionally he tries his hand at something more ambitious than a song. Besides writing *Scenario for Orchestra*, he has also composed *Portrait for Orchestra: Mark Twain*, on a commission by André Kostelanetz. But he is not altogether happy in the larger forms, nor by any means at his best. Essentially he is the creator of cameos. Though these are for popular consumption, they nevertheless reveal the hand of a true artist.

♪♪

RODGERS AND HART

It is a long and devious road that stretches from the sophistication of the *Garrick Gaieties* (1925) to the folk-lore overtones of *Oklahoma!* (1943). In traversing that road Richard Rodgers has proved himself to be one of the most successful composers for the theater in our time. His success is formidable enough when we remark that he has written scores for more than thirty excellent productions, many of them ranking with the leading successes in the American theater; when we realize that hardly a season has passed since 1925 without at least one Rodgers score (and sometimes three or four) brightening the corners of Broadway; when we list even a few of the thousand or so songs that these scores have yielded—"Ten Cents a Dance," "I've Got Five Dollars," "With a Song in My Heart," "My Heart Stood Still," "Thou Swell," and so on.

But if in such achievements he finds worthy equals in men like Kern, Berlin, and Cole Porter, in one respect Rodgers stands alone. When through more studied inspection we learn the infinite variety of theatrical subjects to which he has been forced to adapt his musical gifts, his success achieves a unique distinction. The plays for which he has written music span the distance that separates a circus show (*Jumbo*) and a modernization of Shakespeare (*The Boys from Syra-*

cuse). He has been commissioned to write scores for comedies about the American Revolutionary War (*Dearest Enemy*), about King Arthur's Round Table (*A Connecticut Yankee*), about the ballet (*On Your Toes*), and about politics (*I'd Rather Be Right*)—to mention only a few of his many successes. With the native flexibility of a chameleon he has changed his colors as a composer with each new setting, and produced music that has been felicitously at one with the subject of the text. Nor has he usually taken the easy way—writing neat set numbers that could be used anywhere with equal fitness. Always passionately determined to make his songs an integral part of the play —growing out of the texture of the situation rather than superimposed on it—he has written in the style most appropriate to his subjects. Numbers like the dream sequence and the musical dialogue in *I Married an Angel*, "Sweet Geraldine" from *America's Sweetheart*, "The Lady Is a Tramp" from *Babes in Arms*, or the "March of the Clowns" from *Jumbo*— these songs are not only very good in themselves when set apart from the play, but are integral parts of the plays in which they appear, reflecting the moods and atmospheres which the dramatist has tried to create in his text. Each of these numbers is radically different from any other, both in the idiom of the music and in the manner of its development; to transfer any Rodgers song from one play to another—as is often done with songs in musical comedies—is not to be considered.

Nowhere has Rodgers more conspicuously demonstrated his remarkable flexibility and resiliency than in his score for *Oklahoma!* The play called for simple

RICHARD RODGERS

and unpretentious music modeled after the patterns of American folk songs. What was needed here was not brilliance, nor smartness, nor sentimentality, nor wit. The music to express this authentically American play had to have a definitely established American character—and a character of the West rather than of New York. Shedding his former mannerisms as he would a cloak, Rodgers struck for a new and studied simplicity in song writing. The simplicity of its line and design followed the pattern of the American folk music of the West. And he wrote pieces like "Oh, What a Beautiful Morning, " "Out of My Dreams," "All Or Nothin' "—the most difficult kind of popular song to write, for their appeal comes exclusively from a graceful, unaffected, and unhackneyed lyricism.

Oklahoma! has proved what other, and earlier, scores have long suggested: Rodgers' versatility is of incomparable scope in the popular music of our time. He can write a tender tune with the best of them as evidenced by songs like "My Heart Stood Still," "Blue Moon," and "With a Song in My Heart." He can also by turns be sophisticated and homey, witty and sentimental. But whatever attitude is required of him, he adopts easily, responding to the demands of his text. His music has been of such variety over a period of two decades that it is impossible to single out any one distinctive feature or group of features that may be said to constitute his compositorial style. That failure to assert a recognizable and identifying personality in his music would have been a fatal shortcoming in the concert hall. But in the theater it is precisely the quality which gives him the stamp of greatness.

2.

He has, of course, profited by the greatest single advantage a song composer can know: the collaboration of an ideal lyrist. Temperamentally, the late Lorenz Hart (who died toward the end of 1943) was his opposite. Rodgers is comparatively placid and self-contained, has a well-ordered and disciplined mind. Hart was volatile, fiery, inflammable; he appeared to be traveling in many different directions. The composer worked according to schedule, was methodical, and could always be depended upon to fulfill an assignment with despatch and punctuality. The lyrist worked by fits and starts (usually having to be cornered to complete a given task), writing down snatches of ideas on slips of paper which he crumpled into his pockets.

But the two men had one thing in common: a natural facility for writing. They could produce quickly and easily—without sweat and tears—and with a neatness of construction that never betrayed haste.

There is in a Rodgers-and-Hart song such give-and-take between lyric and melody—the one echoing the subtlest suggestions of the other—that a comparison with Gilbert and Sullivan has inevitably and often been posed. The American duo reminds us of the Savoy pair in the glibness with which they produced their songs, and in the unanimity between lyric and melody. Certainly, Hart's fleet lyrics at their best have the Gilbertian tongue-in-the-cheek mockery. Hart's lyrics—with their sophisticated tone and masterly versification—swept an invigorating fresh breeze through the fetid atmosphere of Tin Pan Alley in the middle 1920's. One has merely to quote from the earliest of Hart's efforts to recognize at once what a long step he took away from the stilted rhyming and the platitudinous metaphors of the lyrics of the time:

> We'll go to Greenwich
> Where modern men itch
>   to be free. . .

Or:

> Beans could get no keener re-
> Ception in a beanery . . .

Or:

> I'll go to hell for ya
> Or Philadelphia. . .

These are all early examples of Hart—long before he hit his full stride as the outstanding lyrist of our times. Yet, compared with the lyric writing with which Tin Pan Alley had satisfied itself for so long a time, it was definitely an evolution out of the dark ages and into civilization.

Lorenz Hart, descended from a branch of Heinrich Heine's family, attended Columbia University where he soon proved his capability for writing smart verse. He did not remain long at Columbia, and soon found a job as translator and adapter of plays from the German. (One of the plays he translated and rewrote was Molnar's *Liliom* for which, despite its great Broadway success, Hart never received any credit.)

When they met for the first time, Hart was twenty-three, and Rodgers sixteen. A friend of both had realized that Hart was a lyrist without a composer, and Rodgers a composer without a lyrist. He thought the two should get together and talk things over, with the possibility of working together. They met, talked all evening about the theater, and clicked. "It was," Rodgers will tell you, "love at first sight." Though the question of collaboration had never once come up during that conversation, both knew—when they separated at the end of the evening—that they were destined to go together, if destined to go anywhere at all.

3.

Richard Rodgers, the son of a physician, was born in New York City on June 28, 1902. From his mother, a competent pianist, he inherited his love of music, and from her he received his first piano lessons. He was naturally musical, able to play the piano by ear when four years old, and inventing little melodic strains of his own before he could even speak coherently. Later, when he studied the piano seriously, he would spend many of his hours of practice in improvising original melodies. At fourteen he wrote his first song—"My Auto Show Girl." Soon he was writing the music for shows produced by a social club of which his brother was a member.

Like Hart, Rodgers entered Columbia and, also like Hart, his college days were brief. Meanwhile he met Hart, and together they decided to write the lyrics and music of the Columbia Varsity Show. Performed in the Grand Ballroom of the Hotel Astor, the show was a tremendous success, and whetted the appetites of the younger men for more. They wrote a song called

"Any Old Place" which was later interpolated in a show, *A Lonely Romeo,* featuring Lew Fields. Other songs followed. The authors went the rounds of Tin Pan Alley, trying to market their songs. Everywhere they were met with polite rejections.

Hart went back to his translation work. Rodgers entered the Institute of Musical Art where, as a pupil of Frank Damrosch, Henry Krehbiel, and George Wedge, he acquired greater technical self-assurance. He was, as a matter of fact, one of the most gifted of the Institute's pupils and was commissioned to write the music for its annual production. (Many years later the one-time student of the Institute was to write a ballet score, *Ghost Town,* a one-act opera, and a symphonic tone poem; but his place, as he himself knows well, is not in Carnegie Hall, but in the Broadway theater.)

After three years at the Institute Rodgers returned to popular music. With Larry Hart he continued to write amateur shows for churches, synagogues, schools, clubs—any place, for that matter, that had a stage, footlights, and a need for entertainment. It was obvious to both men that they were getting nowhere, in spite of their activity. In 1925, after seven years of collaboration, they were no nearer Tin Pan Alley or the Broadway stage than they had been when they wrote the Varsity show. They had written a few complete musical comedies (with books provided by Herbert Fields), but there was not a producer who seemed interested in them. They even tried their hand at legitimate playwriting—*The Melody Man,* which actually saw a Broadway production; but that had been a failure. It was then that Rodgers decided to call the whole thing off. He would get himself an honest man's job in the children's underwear business, and possibly make his way in the world of business, if not in the theater.

The story of how, suddenly, Rodgers and Hart became successful has since become one of the favored sagas of the Broadway theater. The Junior Group of the Theater Guild was planning a little satirical revue to raise funds with which to buy tapestries for the new Guild Theater. The revue was in need of a smart composer and lyrist. Ben Kaye telephoned Rodgers to ask whether he would like the assignment. There was no fee attached, but there was some prospect that the right pair would attract attention. To Rodgers— the none-too-proud father of some twenty-five amateur shows—the chance of writing still another one without benefit of royalties did not seem to be exactly the knock of opportunity. But he let himself be convinced that the writing of music for a show sponsored by the Theater Guild was quite different from anything he had previously attempted.

Hart and Rodgers set to work, and their numbers were incorporated into the Guild production, *Garrick Gaieties*. Originally the revue was scheduled for a single Sunday evening performance, but this proved so successful that a second performance was announced for the following week. This, in turn, brought on a few special matinees to which critics were invited. The raves of the reviewers brought a veritable stampede to the box office. *Garrick Gaieties* was put on a regular run—and it ran for a year and a half.

From that moment on the once reluctant producers beat a track to Rodgers' door. *Dearest Enemy*, which had been written a year before the *Gaieties,* was put on and was successful. Rodgers and Hart found more assignments waiting for them than they could handle—and, with the extraordinary energy now generated by success, they could handle quite a program. In 1926 they had three shows running on Broadway simultaneously; and in 1927, several in London. In rapid succession they followed one success with another: *"The Girl Friend* (1926), *Peggy Ann* (1926), *A Connecticut Yankee* (1927), *She's My Baby* (1927), *Present Arms* (1928), *Spring Is Here* (1928), *Heads Up* (1929), *Simple Simon* (1930), *America's Sweetheart* (1931), *Jumbo* (1935), *On Your Toes* (1936), *Babes in Arms* (1937), *I'd Rather Be Right* (1937), *I Married an Angel* (1938), *The Boys from Syracuse* (1938), *Too Many Girls* (1939), *Pal Joey* (1941), and *By Jupiter* (1942). The Rodgers and Hart touch seemed golden because they were consistently good theater, consistently fresh and new, consistently generous with surprise. Nor was their success confined exclusively to Broadway. In 1930 began their long and financially profitable association with Hollywood—beginning with a score for the Maurice Chevalier film *Love Me Tonight*—an association which has produced more than a dozen excellent scores for the talking screen.

Rodgers' capacity to surprise his audiences persisted even when, in 1943, he ventured on his own for the first time—without the benefit of Hart's collaboration. *Oklahoma!,* the first venture of the Theater Guild into the realm of musical comedy (*Garrick Gaieties* had been a revue—and even then the production of the Junior Group; Gershwin's *Porgy and Bess* was an opera) , provided Rodgers with new scope and horizon —away from sophistication and smartness to the homely simplicities and native flavors of American folklore. It is now well known how successfully Rodgers met this challenge. With admirable lyrics provided by Jerome Kern's lyrist, Oscar Hammerstein 2nd, *Oklahoma!* sounded an altogether new tone for the American musical theater, and for it Rodgers has written his most original music.

♪♪♪

COLE PORTER

In the writing of suave and sophisticated melodies no one has proved Cole Porter's superior. Others may have sounded a deeper and more personal note; others may have been more versatile. But in his own limited sphere, he is without an equal. The tone of his best songs is decidedly Park Avenue, just as his technique is slick French Riviera. Never expressing himself personally (in true sophisticated manner he has avoided any display of excess feeling), he has nevertheless struck an attitude of his own. As elegant in his melodic speech as he is in his everyday address, he has given his songs an identity of their own. There is no mistaking the author of such earlier songs as "What Is This Thing Called Love?," "Love for Sale," "Night and Day," or such later efforts as "Begin the Beguine," "Everything I Love," and "You'd Be So Nice to Come Home to." There is no mistaking the rhythmic heart-throb that pulses in the background of these songs, cogently and irresistibly; nor their broad lyric sweep (usually in a minor-key mood, sometimes touched with Slavic colors), which frequently progresses so effectively to exciting climaxes. With Porter, a new dashing note of smartness entered the popular song. If his songs are less moving or touching than the best of, say, Gershwin or Berlin, they cannot be said to lack either charm or fascination.

169

Like Jerome Kern, Porter is a native son of the Broadway theater, and for the theater he has written his most beguiling music, producing a long series of uninterrupted successes which attest his inventiveness and ingenuity. In the best sense of the continental operetta composers of yesterday, he has the capacity to write tailor-made for dramatic specifications. This is, of course, a gift quite apart from that of writing good songs. It calls for glibness of ideas, facility of expression, and adaptability to different moods. Even when Porter's songs are less noteworthy for originality, they serve the purposes of the theater handsomely. They always have pace: nothing falls quite so flat in the theater as a static melody. They have variety. Taken apart from the context of the play, some of his melodies may at times appear humdrum; but in the theater they bring down the house, because they fill the momentary requirement so completely.

Berlin and Gershwin worked their way up to the heights of success in Tin Pan Alley from humble origins. But Cole Porter, who inherited wealth and married into Blue Book society, can be said to have worked his way down to Tin Pan Alley from Park Avenue. To hear him discuss his career is to appreciate that the struggle to achieve the goal is no less difficult from whichever direction you may come. Broadway producers looked upon Cole Porter and his musical aspirations with suspicion. They regarded him as a playboy of the social world, and were reluctant to entrust to him any major assignment. They considered his musical ambitions merely as the idle day-dreaming of a perhaps bored rich boy with nothing better to occupy his time. To them his musical "scribblings"

COLE PORTER

seemed a hobby which he would discard when something more exciting presented itself. The glitter of his wealth blinded them completely to his powerful and original creative gifts and to his very individual idiom. And so the great of Broadway, visiting his drawing room, drank his champagne and chatted with him amiably—but when they needed music for an important production they forgot Porter's address.

And they could hardly be blamed at the time. For one thing, they knew that the discipline demanded for the writing of good popular music comes not from all-night parties, but (usually) from the necessity of earning a living. How could Porter—product of a leisurely life with no restrictions—possibly force himself to the stern work of composition? Beyond this, they also knew that the first musical-comedy score that Porter had written for Broadway—for a play called *America First,* produced in 1915—had been a pretty shabby failure. Two later scores (for *Hitchy-Koo* in 1919, and the *Greenwich Village Follies* in 1924) had been only moderately successful—even though one of the songs from *Hitchy Koo* ("The Old-Fashioned Garden") had found favor with many. Obviously, you may have wealth, but you cannot buy audiences to listen to your music with admiration, nor can you bribe a nation into singing and loving your songs.

What Broadway producers and publishers did not know, however, was that in the early 1920's Cole Porter was maturing musically. Through experiments, and through the absorption of important musical experiences, he had enriched his musical vocabulary to a point where his speech had become cultured, smart, with tones and overtones of its own. What they could not know, either, was that his need to write music was a far more potent compulsion than any imposed by financial necessity; that, driven by this need, he could not remain silent.

2.

Porter had more than a sound musical instinct, a flair for an original turn of phrase, a polished air, and a great deal of temperament in the songs he was writing (and which producers so long ignored). He added to these a comprehensive musical background, the results of intensive study. He was born in Peru, Indiana—on a seven-hundred-acre farm—on June 9, 1892, of wealthy parents. At the age of six he began to study both the violin and the piano. A self-contained youngster who could scarcely adjust himself to the friendship of other boys, he found inexhaustible fascination in music. He not only played, but composed as well. One of his first efforts was an operetta (for which he wrote both the book and the music) called *Song of the Birds,* written in his tenth year. Somewhat later he composed a piece, "Bobolink Waltz," which was accepted for publication by a small Chicago firm. To this day Porter does not know what happened to the piece, for it was never published, nor was the manuscript ever returned.

His academic years were spent at the East Worcester School for Boys, then at Yale University. At Yale he composed several football songs which achieved considerable popularity. Thence he went on to Harvard for the purpose of studying law. After one semester he decided to transfer to the music school. Harvard provided him with a sound musical training, which was brought to completion in Paris, at the Schola Cantorum under Vincent d'Indy.

This training brought him (after preliminary experience) a facility in writing and a command over the means of his expression. He never had much difficulty in saying precisely what he wanted to and in precisely the way he wished. His songs have always appeared effortless, as if written in the white heat of inspiration. The integration of his best songs—his melodic line flows from the first bar to the last with inevitability, unobstructed by awkward or far-fetched transitions—is the unmistakable product of a thorough schooling.

He had always wanted to be a composer, ever since his boyhood efforts; and, despite his sound musical training, he had always aspired to the writing of popular songs. His first ambitious project, the score for *America First,* was an immature and derivative achievement, predestined for failure. That failure upset him so much that—in a theatrical gesture to escape from his heartache—he joined (of all things!) the French Foreign Legion. We have descriptions of Porter marching with the other Legionnaires through desert stretches, a portable piano on his back! When the regiment came to a resting place, he would play songs for the men and entertain them. Eventually he was awarded the Croix de Guerre by the French government—not for bravery, but for his personality and his capacity for friendship.

When the United States entered the first World War in 1917, Porter was transferred to a French artillery school, where he taught French gunnery to American soldiers. It was during this period that he emerged as a full-grown playboy. His luxurious apartment in Paris became the center of a gay night life and of elaborate festivities which attracted the social élite of Europe. In such a setting of elegance, and in the company of the high-born, Porter moved with charm and grace that stamped him the born host. It was during this period, too, that he entered society through his marriage to Mrs. Lee Thomas, the daughter of William P. Lee of Louisville, Kentucky.

After the war Porter wrote a few scores for the theater, which were only moderately successful. But he felt himself to be something of a pariah in Tin Pan Alley—with success and recognition as remote then as they had been in 1915. He was avoided by managers and publishers. He was compelled to derive personal satisfaction by performing songs like "Let's Do It" and "Two Little Babes in the Woods" at fashionable parties, and listening to the praises of such people as Noel Coward, Elsa Maxwell, and the Prince of Wales. Occasionally (though not often) a professional composer or producer would be impressed by the freshness of his style and would honestly tell him that, though his songs were really good, they were uncommercial. What was meant, of course, was that though the workmanship was professional, the ideas were too original, and were developed with too much independence and boldness to please audiences supposedly responsive only to clichés and formulas. That Gershwin, Kern, Berlin, and Rodgers and Hart had already suggested new worlds for the popular song (and had won acclaim for it) did not yet convince these skeptics that success in popular music could possibly be bought with the shining new coin of originality.

The refusal of the professional theater world to listen to him—or, after listening to him, to be convinced that he had a marketable commodity—brought a temporary halt to his creation. He abandoned Broadway for Italy with the expectation of turning from music to painting. While in Venice he met the famous Broadway producer, Ray Goetz, who confided to Porter that he was about to produce a smart musical comedy on Broadway called *Paris,* with his wife, Irene Bordoni, as star. Goetz had had Martin Brown write the book, and he now wanted a score—of a kind he was sure could not be had from Tin Pan Alley. It must be light, frothy, continental music written in the American jazz idiom. In Tin Pan Alley, Goetz felt, they were too heavy-handed for such delicacies; while in Europe, the leading composers of light music did not understand the psychology of American audiences.

Porter suggested that he could write such a score. Perhaps out of desperation rather than hope, Goetz encouraged him to produce a few samples. Such an assignment was, of course, tailor-made for Porter's talent. Half his life had been spent in the capitals of Europe, and nobody in Tin Pan Alley could be expected to know the continental mannerisms of song-writing better than he. Beyond this, he was temperamentally suited for the writing of music in a suave, Parisian style; *finesse* came naturally to him whether in selecting clothes or in writing music. The samples he showed Goetz proved impressive enough to encourage Goetz to commission the entire score from him. This was in 1928. *Paris* owed no small measure of its great Broadway success to Porter's sprightly and intriguing music.

In 1928 Porter also wrote the music for *Wake Up and Dream*, following this a year later with his score for *Fifty Million Frenchmen*. The *Gay Divorcée* (1932), *Anything Goes* (1934), *Jubilee* (1935), *Red, Hot, and Blue* (1936), *Leave It to Me* (1938), *Du Barry Was A Lady* (1939), *Panama Hattie* (1940), *Let's Face It* (1941), *Something for the Boys* (1942), and *Mexican Hayride* (1944), have provided eloquent testimony that the playboy from Park Avenue has the magic formula for success in popular music. His scores have proved to be an inexhaustibly rich mine, yielding the shining nuggets of song hits in seemingly endless quantities.

Perhaps the most astonishing feature of Porter's productivity—and its consistently high musical level—is that it is achieved through the enervating activity of a playboy's life. Every evening in the week, with few exceptions, Porter makes a round of parties until the early hours of dawn. Sometimes, between dawn and morning, he snatches enough sleep to revitalize him. Then follow business appointments, and luncheon and cocktail dates. A brief rest and careful dress prepare him for another evening of festivity. Further, there are his numerous hobbies, which he follows passionately, to crowd further an already well-filled schedule: hunting, swimming, travel, sports.

Just to make it more complicated, Porter's playboy activities used to be conducted on a global scale. Before 1939 he had a home in Paris, a villa in Venice, and an estate on the Riviera, together with his penthouse atop the Waldorf-Astoria in New York. These were the settings for his year-round social pastimes. Beyond this, he might (on any given day in the calendar) have been just as readily found cruising the South Seas on a yacht, or navigating the Nile, or exploring Africa on horseback, or absorbing Italian sun on the Lido. He was unquestionably the most productive peripatetic composer in history, until history (and Mr. Schickelgruber) confined him within the boundaries of the United States.

At least one secret of his capacity to write so much, and so well, without neglecting either his night life or his daytime hobbies, lies in his excellent compositorial technique and his remarkable powers of concentration. He does not compose at the piano, or with pen on paper, even when he is in the quiet of his own study. He prefers to close his eyes and to do his composing mentally. Frequently he can produce an entire song, correct in every detail, during this period of concentration; putting it down on paper then becomes merely a simple routine either for himself or his secretary. He has composed delectable tunes in the midst of noisy parties—slumping in a soft chair and covering his eyes with the palm of his hand. The entire score of *Anything Goes* was composed aboard a ship moving down the Rhine—the work of composition proceeding while Porter was stretched lazily on a cushioned couch on deck. Not even discomfort—or, worse still, pain—can weaken his powers of concentration: the music for *Leave It to Me* was written while Porter was on crutches, suffering agonizing pain from fractures of both legs.

CHAPTER NINE

BENNY GOODMAN
RAYMOND SCOTT

"It Don't Mean A Thing If It Ain't Got Swing . . . ."

BENNY GOODMAN

♪

BENNY GOODMAN

Like a ceaseless pendulum our popular music has swung between the poles of action and reaction. Ragtime came into vogue as a revolt against the over-sentimental balladry of the 1890's and 1900's. Then Paul Whiteman's "sweet" music developed in reaction against ragtime. Presently, "sweet" music turned saccharine with Rudy Vallee's crooning and the lush choiring of orchestras like Guy Lombardo's. Next, the public's taste veered sharply in still another direction, this time toward swing.

When it first emerged into national prominence soon after 1935, swing encouraged so many analytical dissertations that some persons tended to regard it as something either new or revolutionary. What it proved to be, instead, was little more than New Orleans ragtime with a new name and some added refinements. The very word had been commonly used among musicians for years before it entered general parlance; and Duke Ellington had written a song entitled "It Don't Mean a Thing If It Ain't Got Swing" some four years before swing became a fad.

What is of prime importance to bear in mind—though it is too often ignored—is that swing is *not* an idiom in composition, despite all published attempts to explain its rhythmic and contrapuntal techniques. Its real meaning is evident in the word itself: it is the antithesis of music that is prepared, planned, and designed in advance, and put down on paper before being played. Strictly speaking, therefore, swing is a style of *performance*, and the direction to "swing" a theme is an order to the *performer*. Its most significant element is that free improvisation by solo instruments which, as we have seen in previous chapters, was one of the hallmarks of New Orleans ragtime; and, like that ragtime, its most intriguing feature is the effect of spontaneity engendered by this improvisation. But there is a difference, too: the New Orleans performances consisted exclusively of improvisations, the player never referring to any printed music but relying solely on his instinct and inclination; whereas in swing the improvisation is incorporated within the framework of the printed arrangement—although the latter is made flexible enough to permit individual expression on the part of the solo instruments.

Improvisation, depending as it does on the inspiration of the moment, can be very good or very bad, depending usually on the stimulus of the surroundings, the public, the magnetic powers of fellow performers. When the spark that ignites the musician's imagination is not there, improvisation can be (and frequently has been) pedestrian stuff, dull, artificial, forced. But, as has been said by Hugues Panassie, high priest of the cult of "hot" jazz, at its best jazz improvisation can be of a "beauty far surpassing that of any composed music." "The composer who works cold," argues Mr. Panassie with a great deal of justification, "may have sublime ideas, but only with difficulty can he achieve the heights reached in a collective improvisation where several musicians express themselves in a perfect community of inspiration, playing with a warmth which can be equaled with difficulty by the best interpretation of a written work. . . . In the final analysis, however, the greatest advantage of improvisation over the written composition is the fact that conception and execution are inseparable. While improvising at will—and no jazz musician fails to do so—the musician can create not only from ideas which come to mind but is inspired by the *fashion* in which he is playing."*

Swing freed popular music from the restrictions of formal and unvarying arrangements to which (after the vogue for Whiteman music had reached its height) it had become more and more enslaved. Good arrangements brought discipline to a headstrong and ungovernable music; but it was possible to overdo a very good thing until it became an abuse. Swing brought back independence to part writing and instrumentation in the jazz idiom. It again placed emphasis on solo passages. But none of this, we must repeat, was especially new for 1935. "Before swing became so well liked," wrote Gene Krupa, "it was not uncommon to hear three or four musicians filling in with musical interludes then called 'jam sessions,' simply giving free expression to the rhythms as they caught them. The effects took on a resultant 'kick.' Later, in ensemble work, the importance of this effect was grasped, and became incorporated in the beat and expression of the entire band arrangements."†

While swing was undoubtedly meant for dancing—

---

* Hugues Panassie, *The Real Jazz*, (New York: Smith & Durrell, 1942).
† In a symposium on swing in *Who's Who in Music*, 1942 edition. Lee Stern Press.

and produced that terpsichorean fanatic thenceforth known as the "jitterbug"—it could also be listened to with pleasure. It called upon the jazz performer for the highest virtuosity, the most extraordinary skill and imagination in developing and elaborating given subjects. It drew richly from counterpoint, rhythm, instrumentation. It was, structurally, more complex than Whiteman's music, and required a higher degree of musical sophistication on the listener's part for understanding and appreciation. Its variety of speech, its frequent ingenuity in elaborating ideas, and its glorification of stunningly effective solo virtuosity inevitably created for it a large and devoted public which soon made of it a musical religion.

The popularity of swing can be only partly explained in terms of public reaction against over-sweet music—though that, I feel sure, was a major influence. The repeal of prohibition had opened bars in hotels, night clubs, and restaurants, and alcoholic stimulants undoubtedly made the music of swing more appealing to patrons than its more sober and sedate predecessor had been. There was a great demand throughout the country for small jazz ensembles to fill spots in the newly opened and garishly decorated night clubs and cafés. Many years of propaganda on the part of enthusiasts of "real" jazz or "hot" jazz—not only in this country but even in Europe through the agency of "hot disc" clubs—finally shattered the indifference and skepticism of the general public.

Perhaps most important of all in popularizing swing was the emergence of a brilliant ensemble of white performers (that they were white was also a factor in

making their music palatable to larger audiences).
This ensemble—no one need now be told that it was
Benny Goodman's—preached the gospel of swing with
magnetic effect. Goodman's great swing band did not,
of course, create swing any more than Irving Berlin
created ragtime or Paul Whiteman jazz. But Goodman's ensemble took advantage of the fact that the stage
was set for the appearance of swing and that the zero
hour was at hand.

· 2.

Swing first came to the attention of the entire country in 1935. On November 6 of that year Benny Goodman and his band began an engagement at the Congress Hotel in Chicago. In the announcing advertise-
ments, his was called a swing band—the first public use
of the word in connection with a jazz ensemble.* The
following month Benny Goodman gave a concert of
hot jazz—or swing as it is now called—in the Urban
Room of the Congress Hotel. It was in reporting this
event that *Time Magazine* crowned Goodman the
"King of Swing."

The reign proved prosperous. Over the air, in the
movies, and at the Hotel Pennsylvania in New York,
the swing music of Benny Goodman became a national
passion. In March, 1937, he and his band made a public appearance at the Paramount Theater in New York.
As early as seven o'clock in the morning, hundreds of
youngsters began to form a line to the box office.

---

* Some months earlier, on January 1, 1935, the journal *Down Beat* had
used the term "swing" for the first time to describe improvised melodic
rhythm.

Within an hour, ten mounted policemen were at hand to keep the swelling crowds in line. No sooner had the doors of the theater opened than it was filled to capacity, and the fire department ordered the doors closed again—leaving many thousands waiting outside for the next performance. When, finally, Benny Goodman and his band appeared on the stage, pandemonium broke loose in the theater; it was a spontaneously enthusiastic reception such as no popular music idol had ever before received. Young couples began dancing in the aisles. Loud voices shouted approval of the music and began clamoring for more of it. By the end of the day more than twenty-one thousand excited patrons had paid their way into the theater to hear Goodman.

Benny Goodman's great popularity inevitably inspired the formation of other brilliant swing ensembles by such outstanding jazz performers as Artie Shaw, Tommy Dorsey, Bob Crosby, Chick Webb, and numerous others. In 1938 a Carnival of Swing was held at Randall's Island (in East River, New York) during which twenty-five thousand jitterbugs danced for almost six hours to the music of twenty-five swing bands. Swing records sold in fabulous numbers. Swing music dominated the air waves. In January, 1938, the first swing concert in a concert auditorium took place at Carnegie Hall in a performance by Benny Goodman and his band. "When Mr. Goodman entered," reported Olin Downes in the *New York Times,* "he received a real Toscanini send-off from the excited throng. It took some minutes to establish quiet. There was some quivering excitement in the air, an almost electrical effect. . . . The audience broke out before the music stopped, in crashing applause and special salvos as one or another of the heroes of the orchestra rose in his place to give his special and ornate contribution to the occasion."

Swing, once the cult of the few, was now a national disease. The director of the New York School of Music prepared a special bill for legislation to make its performance illegal.

Benny Goodman's formative years were spent in Chicago, where he heard (and assimilated) the true jazz style as promulgated by some of the leading jazz stylists of the day. He was born in the slums of Chicago in 1909. His father was a tailor who could hardly earn enough to feed his large brood adequately, or to provide them with enough coal or clothing to protect them from the winter cold. Of his father, Goodman has spoken with touching tenderness in his autobiography. He has described with what self-abnegation and devotion the old man consecrated himself to his family. He would be the first to rise so that he might prepare breakfast for his children. Then, after a hard day's work, he would do all the essential shopping for the next day's meals. Asking nothing for himself, never complaining of his fate, Benny's father brought the warmth of his great love and solicitude into a household made drab and chill by poverty.

Benny's father had a profound respect for learning, culture, the arts. He was determined to bring these to his children at any cost. Bitterly he objected to afternoon jobs for his children (even though the coins they might bring into the household were sadly needed!), insisting that their only duty to him was to educate themselves into a better life. The family might be compelled to dispense with milk or meat, but Benny's father was determined that they should not be denied culture.

It was because of his father that Benny turned to music at an early age. The old man had heard that at the neighborhood synagogue there was a boys' band, admission to which entitled the boys to musical training. He took his three sons by the hand and enrolled them for membership in the ensemble. The oldest brother was assigned a tuba, the next in age a trumpet, and Benny, because he was the smallest, a clarinet. Patiently the father led his children to the synagogue each week for rehearsals, and stubbornly he insisted on their practicing their lessons each day.

The synagogue band was discontinued after one year because of lack of funds. Father Goodman searched the corners of Chicago for another similar opportunity for his children. He learned that a musical group was being organized at Hull House which provided instruments, instruction, and uniforms. During the entire winter Father Goodman dragged his children by sled to rehearsals so that they might be spared walking the distance with their instruments.

When Benny was twelve years old, a phonograph entered the Goodman living room—at how great a sacrifice on the part of the father, the children were never to know. Benny now became acquainted with ragtime. His first idol was Ted Lewis, to whose recordings he listened so often that before long he was able to give a reasonable imitation of Lewis' clarinet style. He exhibited this imitative talent at an amateur "jazz night" at the Central Park Theater, and did so well that a few weeks later the manager called upon him to substitute for an absent vaudeville act, and paid him five dollars for his help.

He continued to study the styles of great jazz bands on his phonograph, particularly that of the New Orleans Rhythm Kings. He also went on learning the clarinet with Franz Schoepp, his only formal teacher, and playing it in the band. For diversion he would gather a few boys from the Hull House band and wander off to the woods, where for hours they would hold jam sessions on the popular tunes of the day. He also became the friend of other jazz enthusiasts like himself—fellows like Jimmy McPartland, Frank Teschmaker, and Bud Freeman, each of whom was soon to enrich Chicago jazz with his own talent—and together they would make music and dream about the future.

And the boy grew older. By 1923 he was the proud owner of a union card—his badge of professionalism. He was now able to fill random engagements in and near Chicago. At the same time he haunted most of the famous night spots in Chicago, and studied the jazz idioms of Chicago's greatest men of popular music: Johnny Dodds, King Oliver, Freddie Keppard, Louis Armstrong.

In 1924 he got his first important job. Ben Pollack, a graduate of the New Orleans Rhythm Kings, organized a white band devoted to hot jazz playing—combining the best traditions of New Orleans and Chicago. He gathered the best available instrumentalists in Chicago and with them Benny Goodman, then only sixteen years old. For several years Goodman worked in Pollack's band (his most comprehensive training to date in jazz performance), playing in hotels, on the road, for phonograph records. He was making money;

BENNY GOODMAN 189

and he was acquiring a reputation. But the profits of commercialism did not deflect him from his enthusiasm for and interest in the purest jazz playing. His favorite diversion was joining a few of his friends in impromptu jazz sessions in which—musically speaking—they could go to town, unhampered by commercial requirements or the tastes of audiences. "The best-known hangout for musicians was a little hole-in-the-wall called the Three Deuces on State Street," Goodman recalls in his autobiography.* "The room downstairs, where they jammed, was a dismal, unpainted place, with wooden walls, and no covering on the floor. Over on one side was an old beaten-up piano. Sometimes when you'd go in there sober, it almost knocked you off your feet. If the boys were going good, you'd just as apt as not to see the other fellows beating the rhythms on the walls with their hands when somebody took a chorus. . . . I remember one session that began about two in the morning and lasted well into the bright daylight hours, when Ben Pollack sat in on the drums, and I played clarinet. Then there was a terrific one a little later on when the Whiteman band was at the Chicago Theater, when Tommy Dorsey came down and sat in with Glenn [Miller], Tesch, Condon, Bix [Beiderbecke], and Krupa who was beginning to play good drums at that time."

3.

In 1928 Goodman came to New York with Ben Pollack's orchestra to fill an engagement at the Little Club

* Benny Goodman (with Irving Kolodin), *The Kingdom of Swing*, Harrisburg: Stackpole Sons, 1939).

on 44th Street off Broadway. The engagement was not successful, and until others came his way, things were hard for the young clarinetist. He tells of being compelled to steal milk bottles from the halls of his rooming place so as to turn them in for their deposit refunds. Occasionally there was a job, as, for example, at the Million Dollar Pier in Atlantic City, or in the pit of a Broadway musical comedy, *Hello, Daddy*. But lean periods usually followed the fat ones.

A personal quarrel between Goodman and Pollack decided Goodman to become a free-lance. He played in numerous theater orchestras (including several George Gershwin shows), made records (frequently with small ensembles), and filled some engagements over the air. His popularity increased slowly. Meanwhile he nursed a great ambition which made it possible for him to endure stoically the vacillations of fortune: he would start a band of his own, and with that band would play jazz music the way he had always felt it should be played, regardless of the preferences of his public. He would satisfy his own soul—not sell it for a price.

In 1934 a recording contract given him by Columbia enabled him to organize his first ensemble, and his earliest records with this group were "Basin Street Blues," "Riffin' the Scotch," and "Georgia Jubilee." A brief engagement at Billy Rose's Music Hall followed. Gradually other assignments came along. Then he got a toehold in radio, when the National Biscuit Company, deciding to sponsor a program featuring three bands— sweet music, hot music, and rhumba—chose Goodman's group to play the hot music. Improved by Fletcher Henderson's arrangements and by the addition of drummer Gene Krupa to the ensemble, Goodman's music was now carried from coast to coast over a network of fifty-three stations. And though he did not know it, that music was being heard and admired by lovers of real jazz throughout the country, who were later to form the nucleus of his rabid devotees.

A coast-to-coast tour, during which he played mostly in dance halls, eventually took Goodman and his band to the Palomar in Los Angeles. During the trip he had been playing hot music to indifferent audiences; and he therefore decided now to compromise with his integrity and alter his style somewhat to meet the popular taste of the moment for sweet music. But this proved hardly more acceptable than the hot had been, and by the time he reached the Palomar he decided that if he *was* to be a failure, he would at least be a failure in his own way and according to his own conscience. He called for his most brilliant Henderson arrangements and told his musicians that they could play as hot as they wished. They played—obviously from the depths of their hearts—played in defiance of their disappointments and their fears for the future. From the texture of this music rose Goodman's clarinet in improvisations embellished by magic figurations. "To our complete amazement, half of the crowd stopped dancing and came surging around the stand. It was the first experience we had had with that kind of attention, and it certainly was a kick. That was the moment that decided things for me. After traveling three thousand miles, we finally found people who were up on what we were trying to do, prepared to take our music. . . . The first big roar from the crowd was one of the sweetest sounds I ever heard in my life—and from that time on the night kept getting bigger and bigger, as we played about every good number in the book."

And now success followed success. An excellent booking at the Congress Hotel in Chicago proved so sensational (he had been engaged for six weeks, but he remained for seven months) that it was succeeded by a desirable engagement at the Hotel Pennsylvania in New York. The crowds came in increasing numbers to hear his music, and they responded to it zestfully. There was drive, rhythmic propulsion, an exciting kinesthetic appeal in the sounds that his band released so lavishly; and they proved irresistible. Beyond this, there was Goodman's clarinet—that extraordinary technical command of the instrument which has made him as comfortably at home with Mozart and Bartók as with swing—and with it his talent for fanciful jazz developments.

He may not be a particularly magnetic personality on the stage. A bit staid and self-conscious, his mannerisms comparatively formal, he appears (with his spectacles) more like a college teacher or a librarian than a jazz high priest. There is no suggestion of the flamboyant showman about him. Visually he is about as romantic as a grocery clerk. But once he begins making music he is dynamic, and he becomes dynamic because of the luscious pattern of sounds that emerges from his clarinet.

He had arrived—and he had arrived without selling his soul or compromising his ideals. An endless round of engagements now kept him hard at work uninterruptedly during his waking hours. He has carried a staggering burden in filling all the engagements that were asked of him, but he seems to thrive on work and more work. He is never more cheerful than when he has more calls than he has hours in which to fill them. Personal appearances in the theater, important spots on the air (here alone his audience was at one time computed to be about two million a week!), recording dates, engagements at hotels—these bring him an income of more than a hundred thousand dollars a year and have established him as unrivaled "King of Swing." His sovereignty was still accepted in 1943, when the then Undersecretary of State Sumner Welles appointed him to President Roosevelt's Advisory Committee of Music (the only swing master to receive such an honor), the function of which was to stimulate and promote the performances of the music of the Americas in the Americas.

♪♪

RAYMOND SCOTT

Whatever else you may say of Raymond Scott, you cannot accuse him of being unoriginal. A sort of Peter Pan of popular music, he is best characterized by the word "whimsical." He has formed a Quintet that was first composed of six men, later of seven (he called it a Quintet because he liked the sound of the word). Into this ensemble he gathered some of the best available instrumentalists, and then trained them in a freak routine that he called "silent music," in which they went through all the paces of music-making without uttering a tone. He has tried to express in music the "feel" of a thimble, a telephone, a hot ear of corn, and a bumpy air journey over Newark; and he has tried to get musical effects out of such outlandish "instruments" as seashells, barrels of water, wire whisks, and table tops. He has composed jazz pieces with some of the screwiest titles ever concocted—*Duet for Piano and Pistol, The Girl with the Light Blue Hair, Square Dance for Eight Egyptian Mummies, Dinner Music for a Pack of Hungry Cannibals*—and then proceeded to write for these titles music that is outstanding for its inventiveness and seriousness of purpose.

He indulges in the unexpected as naturally as most people resort to the cliché. He arrived at his name, "Raymond Scott," by thumbing through a telephone book. Born Harry Warnow, he refused to capitalize on the success of his brother, Mark Warnow, a famous conductor over the radio. Having composed a musical morsel called *War Dance for Wooden Indians,* based upon "an old Indian legend," he soon confessed that the Indian legend was actually a story of his own creation. At a recent broadcast he announced the première of his latest work, *Two Preludes*—"but I'll only be able to perform the second prelude today," he explained, "because I haven't yet written the first."

To popular music he has come as a fresh figure, a musician who has administered a tonic to a frequently tired and stodgy business. Yet, behind his unique way of expressing himself, we discover no quest for publicity, or for originality for originality's sake. Rather, we find a sound intellect searching restlessly for new directions. His original pieces are not only whimsical; they are at times brilliant projections of hot-jazz styles and idioms which, up to now, had been confined almost exclusively to dance music. His jazz performances are not only novel; they have evolved all sorts of new sound qualities (particularly over the radio microphone) and jazz effects. In his own way, he has done as much for the development of jazz as almost any other single person since Gershwin. And he has only just begun.

In personal contact there is nothing to suggest the quality of whimsy that pervades his music. Of medium height, built rather solidly, dressed in smartly tailored clothes, he gives the effect of a very sound musician, who is sincere, integrated, and honest—and driven by a savage conscience. Whether he talks about himself in the first person or in the third (he sometimes tells you that "Scott does this," or "Scott does that," almost

RAYMOND SCOTT

as if Scott were another person), he is always conscious
that he has an artistic mission to perform. A more or
less seriously trained musician (he spent several years
at a conservatory), he has an almost fanatical belief in
the artistic potentialities of good jazz. "*Real* jazz," he
once said to the present writer, "is a language in itself,
with its own vocabulary, its own idioms, its own accents. This language is important artistically—important because it is American to its very roots and speaks
for America. It is an art in its own right and with
further evolution it will become a major element in
our musical expression. Authentic jazz has a definite
role to fill in good American music. When serious composers begin exploring all the possibilities of jazz (and
by jazz I mean hot jazz), and study it carefully, they
will realize that it offers them new and rich possibilities for artistic self-expression. Equally important, they
will find an audience of millions waiting to hear their
music, millions who are sensitive to it, who understand
it, and who—because they grew up with it—feel that it
is a musical expression of their inmost selves."

By jazz, Scott means not only the jazz rhythms, colors, and harmonies exploited in serious music by such
composers as Gershwin, Grofé, and Morton Gould.
He means materials which are even more indigenous
to jazz, and which up to now have been for the most
part ignored by the serious musician: materials first discovered in New Orleans, then developed by an entire
generation of hot-jazz artists from King Oliver to Duke
Ellington. These materials (we have already commented upon them in preceding chapters) form a rich
language which Scott has tried to absorb within the
texture of his little serious pieces. Scott feels confident

that the same thing can be done for symphony, concerto, and even opera. As a matter of fact, as the first step in this direction, Scott has written a score for ballet called *The Gremlins,* his first large work.

He has always felt that way about jazz. His father, formerly a concert violinist in Russia, owned a record shop in New York. Scott's boyhood was spent playing one jazz record after another. The jazz that interested him even then was not that of the popular tunes of the day, with their comparatively stereotyped patterns and effete sentiments. He went for the hot playing of the jazz artists from New Orleans and Chicago. He would play these hot records again and again, feeling them so personally that, as he explains, "every part of me vibrated with the nervous and excited strains of the wailing trumpets and trombones."

He was born in Brooklyn, in 1909. He attended Brooklyn Technical School, taking six years and a half for the four-year course largely because he discovered a radio laboratory in the school and spent all his time fiddling around with experiments instead of doing his homework. This interest in science has never left him; it is still his pet hobby, his special subjects being acoustics and sound transmission, and reproduction in relation to the radio. He has spent a great deal of time and effort in the study of radio reception and the sounds that can be transmitted over the microphone, and as a result has been able to invent new sound qualities. In order to pursue his studies and experiments at home, he has built for himself an audio laboratory, in which he passes many of his leisure hours.

He is passionately interested in all phases of recording. Everything he writes and everything he plays with his ensemble is put on records; recently he had built in his home, under his own supervision, a special phonograph in which a recording machine is incorporated. These records he studies carefully, dissecting them with microscopic thoroughness, and making improvements and changes. He spends hours listening to the recorded works of the masters, following the full printed score, and studying their form and instrumentation.

Scott enlists machinery even in his composition; using a special apparatus attached to the piano which automatically records on movable tape the final one-minute of piano performance, he will improvise aimlessly at the keyboard, and then—when suddenly he catches a striking mood or a combination of tones—he will listen to the one-minute throwback of his improvisation, and at once transcribe it on paper if he feels it can serve him. He talks now of getting several of these machines for the purpose of experimenting with contrapuntal writing—recording one voice at a time and then playing several tapes simultaneously.

Upon his rather belated graduation from high school, he performed one of his pieces, *Metropolis,* as part of the graduation exercises. He had lately spent a good deal of time improvising on the piano and composing little pieces. His brother, Mark Warnow, detected some signs of talent, and insisted upon further musical training for Scott. So Scott was sent to the Institute of Musical Art, where he remained a few years.

In 1930 he got a job as house pianist for the Columbia Broadcasting System, but he still spent his leisure hours in composing. One of his pieces, *Christmas Night in Harlem,* was featured by brother Mark over the air in 1932. In 1936 Scott was performing with a small jazz group which was soon called upon to fill a spot in the first hot-jazz program on a network, "Saturday Night Swing." The group included the trombonist Jerry Colonna (now the famous comedian), trumpeter Bunny Berigan, and drummer Johnny Williams. Williams joined Scott when, in 1937, Scott decided to go on his own and start his Quintet. The Scott Quintet included—beside its founder and Johnny Williams—Peter Pumiglio (clarinet), Dave Harris (saxophone), Louis Schoobe (bass), and Dave Wade (trumpet).

The Quintet caught on immediately. In April, 1937, it made its first records, and these records sold in hundreds of thousands, rapidly becoming the fastest selling discs on the market. Personal appearances in theaters became, for Scott, occasions of personal triumph. His original pieces (the first that he featured was *Twilight in Turkey*), his novel arrangements, his meticulously prepared performances, all sounded a new note for jazz, and found appreciative audiences in different stratas of society. Serious musicians like Stravinsky and Heifetz became his fans. With them were lovers of good hot jazz throughout the whole country all the way from the Oshkosh jitterbug to Duke Ellington.

A piece he wrote at this time, called *In an Eighteenth Century Drawing Room* (a jazz modernization of the opening theme from Mozart's C-Major Piano Sonata, K. 545), further helped to make him a national figure—and, incidentally, was to some extent responsible for a fresh wave of thefts from the classics. He was called to Hollywood by David Selznick. They did not get along: Scott didn't like the restrictions imposed upon him, he didn't like the costumes he had to wear, above everything else he didn't like being pigeonholed. Darryl Zanuck took over his contract. For Zanuck, Scott wrote music for (and appeared in) pictures starring Eddie Cantor and Shirley Temple. One of the pieces he wrote for Shirley, "Toy Trumpet," became another national hit.

But he didn't like Hollywood, and it was not long before he was back in New York. It was at this time that he created for the Columbia network the first of his jazz laboratories, in which he was permitted to experiment with jazz styles, performances, and instruments to his heart's content. Now he once again has a jazz laboratory over the air—part of a contractual arrangement with Columbia—in which he tries to widen the scope of his own jazz art, as well as to provide an outlet for new jazz works. Jazz may not yet be a full-grown art. Nevertheless, Scott has proved in his laboratory that it can be as deliberate, scientific, sincere, preconceived, and controlled as any other artistic expression. One of the least publicized (but by no means least significant) of his achievements with his laboratory was his success in removing the hokum and phony mystery that has so long surrounded jazz performances and creative people of jazz—and revealed both of them in their true light. Scott's jazz laboratory constitutes the most important encouragement thus far given to hot-jazz art over the radio, and its influence will be strongly felt.

A stickler for accuracy, who is concerned over the slightest detail of performance, Scott drives his men in rehearsal relentlessly before he is satisfied with their playing. Just as he likes his own compositions to be terse, concise, to the point, so in his performances he demands a clean attack, compactness, and the avoidance of superfluities and instrumental excesses. He is a specialist in devising new sound effects, and he is particularly sensitive to the most subtle dynamics and tone shadings. Even as a boy he used to be sent into strange moods by unusual colors, lights, or sounds. Today, one combination of sounds can throw him into despair; another will thrill him. At rehearsals he is always experimenting with timbres, colors, sonorities, pitch deviations, harmonies. He has often said that, though composition is his major interest, he will never abandon his work as a leader of a jazz ensemble because it affords him such enviable opportunities for research, study, and experimentation with jazz materials.

CODETTA

CODETTA

The preceding pages have discussed tools developed during the past forty years—the tools with which our popular music has been created. In those forty years the tools have become functional, flexible. Some day a musical historian will write a book that will carry the story to its logical end, showing how in the meantime craftsmen who are artists, and artists who are craftsmen, will have taken these tools and of them made instruments capable of fashioning art works of real greatness.

I have indulged in the above metaphor for a specific reason. Thus far, the idiom and the styles perfected by our men of popular music are little more than tools sharpened and trued for future use. In experimenting with these tools, certain pioneers have produced works that have become a part of our tradition and that will probably survive for many years. But not yet is our popular music great art. A number of admirable books have been written, true, that seek to prove the artistic importance of our popular music; and there is some validity in their argument. But careful study of the music itself reveals that as yet it represents aspiration' rather than realization. The tools are here—devised, improved, ready, after forty years of experiment; but it is the next forty years that must utilize them in the production of great art.

If we look at the extraordinary development that has taken place in our popular music since 1900—the enrichment of harmonic, rhythmic, and melodic writing; the birth of a new instrumentation; and the growth of a rich vocabulary peculiar to the music itself—can we help feeling confident in its future? When we compare the naïveté and grammar-school simplicity of the sentimental ballads of the late 1890's and the early 1900's with the manifold subtleties and refinements created by George Gershwin, Duke Ellington, and Raymond Scott, we begin to appreciate the progress that popular music has made within our own lifetime.

Today we no longer ask: Will ragtime live? Will jazz live? Will swing live? Will boogie-woogie live? Today we know that what is vital in them has survived and will survive; what is meretricious will lapse into obscurity. That they have enough vitality to serve as the basis of an important musical art has been the argument of this book. Tomorrow should prove the valid conclusions of today's argument just as forcefully and eloquently as yesterday has provided its premises. The story of our popular music has actually only begun.

APPENDIX

BIBLIOGRAPHY

Armstrong, Louis. *Swing That Music.* New York: Longmans, Green & Co., 1936.

Ewen, David. *The Story of George Gershwin.* New York: Henry Holt & Co., 1943.

Goffin, Robert. *Jazz.* Garden City: Doubleday, Doran & Co., 1944.

Goldberg, Isaac. *George Gershwin.* New York: Simon & Schuster, Inc., 1931.

Goldberg, Isaac. *Tin Pan Alley.* New York: John Day Co., 1930.

Goodman, Benny, and Kolodin, Irving. *The Kingdom of Swing.* Harrisburg: Stackpole Sons, 1939.

Handy, W. C. *The Father of the Blues: An Autobiography* (edited by Arna Bontemps). New York: The Macmillan Co., 1941.

Hobson, Wilder. *American Jazz Music.* New York: W. W. Norton & Co., 1939.

Panassie, Hugues. *The Real Jazz.* New York: Smith & Durrell, Inc., 1942.

Ramsey, Frederick, and Smith, C. E. (editors). *Jazzmen.* New York: Harcourt, Brace & Co., 1939.

Sargeant, Winthrop. *Jazz: Hot and Hybrid.* New York: Arrow Editions, Co-operative Association, Inc., 1938.

Smith, Charles E. and others. *The Jazz Record Book.* New York: Smith & Durrell, Inc., 1942.

Whiteman, Paul, and McBride, Margaret. *Jazz.* J. H. Sears & Co., 1926.

Witmark, Isidore, and Goldberg, Isaac. *Story of the House of*

Whitmark: From Ragtime to Swingtime. New York: Lee Furman, Inc., 1939.

Woollcott, Alexander. *The Story of Irving Berlin.* New York: G. P. Putnam's Sons, 1925.

SOME RECOMMENDED RECORDINGS

B—*Brunswick*   D—*Decca*
C—*Columbia*   V—*Victor*

CHAPTER I

New Orleans Jazz. Armstrong, Dodds, and Noone Orchestras. D-Album 144.

CHAPTER II

Irving Berlin Songs. Paul Whiteman Orchestra. D-Albums 70, 71.

CHAPTER III

Chicago Jazz Album. All-Star Personnel. D-Album 121.
Chicago Jazz Classics. Benny Goodman and His Boys. B-1007.
Louis Armstrong. Armstrong and His Hot Five. C-57.
Louis Armstrong. Armstrong and Assisting Artists. C-28.
Bix Beiderbecke. Beiderbecke and Assisting Artists. C-29.
Comes Jazz. Bud Freeman and Famous Chicagoans. C-40.

CHAPTER IV

The Birth of the Blues, an album of W. C. Handy classics. NBC Chamber Music Society of Lower Basin Street. V-P82.
Boogie-Woogie Music. Pete Johnson, Ammons, Meade "Lux" Lewis, and others. D-Albums 137, 235.
Boogie-Woogie. Johnson, Lewis, Ammons, Basie, etc. C-44.

Fletcher Henderson. Fletcher Henderson and His Orchestra. C-30.

A Duke Ellington Panorama. Duke Ellington and His Orchestra. V-P138.

The Duke. Duke Ellington and His Orchestra. C-38.

Paul Whiteman and his orchestra have made numerous single-disc recordings for Columbia; consult catalogue.

George Gershwin Music. Paul Whiteman and His Orchestra. D-Albums 31, 57.

Ferde Grofé's *Grand Canyon Suite.* Kostelanetz and His Orchestra. CM-463.

George Gershwin Music. Paul Whiteman and His Orchestra. D-Album 31. (This album includes *Rhapsody in Blue, Second Rhapsody, An American in Paris, Cuban Overture.*)

Rhapsody in Blue. Boston Pops Orchestra and Sanromá. V-11822-2.

Concerto in F. Boston Pops Orchestra and Sanromá. VM-690.

Porgy and Bess (excerpts). Duncan, Brown, Jessye Choir, etc., and Orchestra under Smallens. D-Albums 145-283.

George Gershwin Songs. Soloists, Orchestra. D-Albums 96, 97.

Show Tunes of Jerome Kern. Al Goodman and Orchestra. C-34.

Kern Melodies. Decca Orchestra. D-Album 232.

Kern Melodies. Gordon String Quartet. D-Album 293.

Rodgers-Hart Comedy Hits. Orchestra under Rodgers. C-11.

Cole Porter. Victor Mixed Chorus. V-P107.

Cole Porter Songs. Mary Martin. C-123.

Benny Goodman has made numerous single-disc recordings for
Columbia; consult catalogue.

Raymond Scott has recorded many of his original pieces for
Decca; consult catalogue.